Morning Gleam. [Frontispiece.]

Page 34.

MORNING-GLEAM:

OR,

THE PASTOR'S DAUGHTER.

Philadelphia:
AMERICAN BAPTIST PUBLICATION SOCIETY,
530 ARCH STREET.

MORNING-GLEAM:

OR,

THE PASTOR'S DAUGHTER.

CHAPTER I.

WHO that has seen much of the world has not at some time beheld a landscape so touchingly beautiful as to awe the soul into silent admiration, as if he were in the presence of Him who drew its wondrous outlines, filled it with light and shade, and then breathed the breath of life upon it? Nor is it the refined, the intellectual, and the wise only, who feel the magic power of Nature on their souls. The rudest peasant finds his very heart growing fast to his native hills, rugged though they be; so that when exiled by poverty or political tyranny, he refuses to be blessed in kindlier scenes, and chooses to nurse the bleeding wound caused by the separation in his homesick bosom. The Switzer, driven for bread to the rich prairies of our happy country, stretches his gaze across the mighty plains in search of one hill to relieve the lonely sameness, but in vain. The corn may wave almost without his toil or care, and bring gold to his coffers; but still the tears will fall for the glorious old mountains of father-land, and in dreams his feet clamber their rugged sides, while in an ecstacy of delight he clasps the high rocks beside the cot of his infancy, and, kissing their rugged cheeks, he vows never, never more to lose sight of "God's hills"—not even for bread—far less for gold. The poor Icelander, after amusing himself with the charms of cultivated nature—the lawn, the park, and the lake—turns around and with eager gaze asks, "But where is the sea?" Even the child loves the outdoor world, and prefers the freedom and beauty of Nature, even in the storm, to the ceiled house; while the tiniest baby, who has not power to speak its joy, claps its little hands and shouts in bird-like notes as it gazes in new wonder on the moon, the stars, or the flower, and the tree.

Let none say that Nature's ministry is confined to the wise: each of God's creatures enjoys in his own measure her teachings, feeling his soul elevated, gladdened, and purified thereby. It was not alone to supply bread for our coarser nature that God made this earth, with its wealth of field and flood; it was not to satisfy our avarice that he reared the mighty hills, filling their deep bosoms with treasures of jewel and mine. Oh, no! He who made man has implanted in the immortal mind deeper longings, which will not, cannot be satisfied with the bread that perisheth, and has also provided food for that appetite. Next to seeing God himself, and talking with him in the word of life, is beholding him in his works and receiving with grateful love the lessons he thus sends us.

The view from Morning-Gleam Cottage was never surpassed by artist's vision wrought out on canvas. On either side were vast and fruitful fields, waving in their season with the golden grain, or velvet pastures, over which the patient herds and happy flocks grazed and sported through the long, glad summer. Below, and stretching off into the far distance, lay a valley whose rich and undulating surface was dotted over by clumps of elms and maples, which reflected their quivering foliage in many a mimic lake that glanced out beneath the sunshine, or vailed its brightness under the cloud.

Behind the cottage, and crowning the hill on whose side it stood, was a grand old forest, whose tall trees stretched out their brawny arms as if to guard and bless the humble dwelling. From the hill-top and also from the upper piazza of the cottage could be seen the noble windings of a glorious New England river, whose praise has been sung by more than one whom God has anointed poet.

The pretty cottage, with its green blinds and its broad portico, stood in the midst of highly cultivated grounds. Passers-by—strangers to the occupant—made many and different comments on the place. Said one, "If I could afford such an elegant garden, I would build a finer house to correspond with it." But he was answered by his companion, "The tall, pale young man you see toiling there does not own either cottage or grounds; nor yet, that I know of, a square foot of land on all God's earth." "Then," replied the other, "he is very unwise; the owner will be made rich by these improvements, but never thank him for his pains."

Farmer Grub, who owned tho next place and who counted every inch of soil as so much money, often shrugged his shoulders and said, "Our parson is not a practical man, or else he'd lay down that 'ere flower-garden to grass, or plow it up and plant it with potatoes, cabbages, and turnips. Why, if I had that piece in my hands, I'd raise all my own garden 'sass' and sell fifty dollars worth a year besides. And then there's that clump o' trees down in the first gully after you go out o' the garden-gate—why, it's three year or more since I got 'em to vote at parish-meetin' to give that to the parson for fire-wood, for I never did think he had enough money; and, don't you believe, he wouldn't have 'em cut, but said he'd rather see 'em standin' than enjoy 'em burnin'. He's a dear, good, faithful man, but he ain't very practical, that's sure."

It was very certain that the pastor, who found early and late his exercise and recreation in that tasteful garden, was cast in another mould from some of his more earthly-souled hearers; but still he was to all intents and purposes an eminently practical man; laboring in season and out of season in every judicious way for the temporal good and the eternal salvation of his beloved flock. He loved the beautiful works of his Father's hand; and every bird, leaf, and flower brought a lesson or whispered comfort to his heart. Thus, while he toiled for health, he received pleasure such as the vain enjoyments of earth have not to offer the sons of folly

Mr. Bond was not a solitary laborer in his garden. Sweet little Maggie, his only child, was up with the lark, running from bed to bed, dropping the tiny seed or plucking the hurtful weed, as her father directed; meanwhile delighting his fond heart with her innocent questions, and her childish yet sage comments.

These were hours of the greatest enjoyment to the child; and although she often went in to her breakfast a little weary, she was more than repaid by the vigor and fresh flow of spirits which followed. The happy thoughts of her heart, the red roses on her cheeks, the music in her soul, but, more than all, the sweet lessons of heavenly love she learned, were thus worth a life of labor. Her tender mind was on these occasions led up to God, our loving Father, who made this earth for our home, and who causeth it to bring forth abundantly every thing for our happiness as well as for our necessity. She loved to hear of God, and to trace his finger in the glorious things around her. All these became the teachers of holy things to her tender mind, and were connected with that clearer word which God has sent us as the interpreter of Nature. Maggie's knowledge of the Scriptures was wonderful for a child of eight years, and every change she saw in the seasons, the heavens, or in vegetation, brought to mind some passage she had learned. Many who knew not the pains by which these things had been implanted in her heart, were amazed at her language, and looked upon it as a kind of inspiration. Some good but superstitious old ladies, after talking with her, would shake their heads mournfully, saying, "That child is not long for this world;" as if God takes all the good and sensible folks out of the world before they have time to work for him and their generation. As in other cases, these prophetesses were widely mistaken in regard to our little heroine, for she did live, as you will see, not only to labor but also to suffer for Christ—to be a burden-bearer in his harvest-field. But that the reader may have some idea of what the prognostications were founded on, we will give a little example of her conversation, much of which was carried from lip to lip, growing as it went, until some who had never seen but only heard of her, thought the child must vie with Solomon for wisdom.

When the sun began to rise in all his glory, and Maggie and her father were at their work, she would say:

"Look now, dear papa, and see if he does not come up as the Bible says, 'like a strong man to run a race.'"

When the happy sparrows circled and fluttered around her home until they reached their own mansion on the high pole far above her little chamber-window, she would gaze earnestly upward and murmur, perhaps to herself: "Not one of them can fall to the ground without your Father." When the lily-buds first began to open, she would whisper almost involuntarily, "Not even Solomon in all his glory was arrayed like one of these." When she looked on the cattle grazing in the pastures she would say, "The cattle upon a thousand hills are mine;" and when she caught from some elevation a glimpse of the winding river, and saw the ripples dancing like silver stars upon its bosom, after her first exclamation of delight, would be heard in softened tones, "There is a river the streams whereof make glad the city of our God."

You will see, dear young reader, that such language and such trains of thought are not common to childhood; for the book of life declares—and all who have the care of the young can testify to its truth—that "folly is bound up in the heart of a child." Thus, as she mingled very little among the people, never attending school, it is not strange that those who saw only the bright side of her character, and heard only her remarkable sayings, should have considered her one "not born for earth." Thrice blessed is that child who is thus made by holy teachings to inherit as its own all the rich and beautiful things of God! She may never hold the deed of one acre of his earth, never have the right to sell one flower, nor to say of one lamb, "It is my own;" and yet they are all hers to enjoy in a purer and nobler sense than can many who are owners of the soil, but whose abundance and the anxious care it brings will not suffer them to sleep.

One of these blessed ones was little Maggie Bond. She enjoyed every moment of daylight, and at nightfall laid her prayer-blessed head on a pillow which was proof against all evil dreams, and slept—shall we say in the love and peace of God? Nay, young and pleasant and wise as was this child of many prayers, she had her anxious hours—her troubled thoughts; for she knew that her heart was not right in the sight of God—that her chief aim in all the little acts of love she performed was not to please him, but those dear friends whom he had given her.

CHAPTER II.

AFTER all the good things we have said of Maggie, some young reader may imagine that she was one of those good children we read about but never see, without one fault or frailty; little stray creatures from the courts above, who never knew sin. Such children are very rare, although those with some faint claim to perfection are now and then met with; but even this is often but the creation of a foolishly fond mother's imagination, or the result of a diseased system. We do sometimes see little ones who seem to have no evil of their own, no desire for childhood's sports, no cup in their heart running over with sparkling merriment; who choose to sit beside their mother all the long day while the bees hum and the birds sing abroad, reading books beyond their comprehension or doing nothing. But such are objects of *pity* rather than of emulation; being either the victims of vain mothers, who, to boast of their precocity, rob them of their childhood—that God-given heritage, or else the subjects of premature decay. Usually, such have large heads with projecting foreheads, full, deep-set, watery eyes, temples thickly lined with blue veins, and limbs too frail to support their body. Poor little unfortunates! They, having never had the health for out-door exercise and play, have learned to talk and think like the older people among whom they pass their time. Like hot-house plants, they are unable to bear the air of out-door life, and incompetent to shed abroad that fragrance which those do who are reared abroad and feel God's breath upon their spirits.

Now Maggie Bond was neither one of these patient little sufferers nipped in the bud, nor yet one of those who, having been flattered and praised for being "little women or little ladies, instead of romps who roll hoops and climb fences," barter away their innocent and artless childhood, with its wealth of joys, for the reputation of being "old and wise." She was a true child, warm-hearted, impulsive, and full of glee. When study and work were over, she might be seen, her curls flying and her sun-browned cheek glowing with roses, chasing the golden butterfly over the lawn, decking with flowers a captive lamb, or arraying in her own bonnet and shawl the demure old cat "Grizzle," or the dog "Bruno" who slept by her side in a most neighborly spirit on the broad kitchen hearth. These last were of no small importance in the little family. Puss was an officer always on duty, having special charge over Maggie's poultry, that no enemy might invade their little camp by night; while Bruno, although given his master for a watch-dog, seemed to understand that, as there was very little to watch, his post was a sinecure, and acted as page, attending Maggie in all her rambles through woodland, marsh, and glen. And a most faithful guide he was, knowing the points of the compass and guessing at the dinner or tea hour with far more accuracy than could she with all her wisdom. He bore all her little gifts to the poor in the village, whether strawberries in a basket or dainty morsel in a pail, never presuming, however near his own dinner-hour, to meddle with that which belonged to another. He was a real treasure to Maggie—protector and playmate.

This free, joyous spirit was encouraged by her parents; for they well knew that children who are happy and busy at their play will carry the same energy into their duties in after-life; and they were striving to rear their daughter, not for a puppet of the ball-room, or the pet of fashionable triflers, but for a missionary of mercy in this sorrowful world. To this end they did not set before her life in all its darkest hues, to frighten her spirit at the threshold, but rather impressed her with the goodness of God, who for every trial he permits, sends us a thousand mercies. They encouraged her buoyancy, and provided, as far as in their power, the means of making her happy, while yet no shadow lay on her pathway. They considered it a religious duty to make home the brightest spot on earth, so that, whatever darkness might await her in the future, she could look back on "the sunny hours of childhood," and hope that, as in the past, so should it be in the future. Home should be made, as far as might be, an emblem of heaven. But to how many little ones is it only the place where they are sheltered, fed, and disciplined? Is it not so in some Christian families, where the injunction to be "sober-minded," is more highly regarded than the command, "Rejoice evermore?"

Not thus was it in the case of Maggie Bond. Home was her paradise, and every room bore evidence that a child dwelt there whose comfort and pleasure were consulted in all the arrangements. True, very little money had been spent in the purchase of toys, but loving hearts and willing hands had in leisure hours more than made amends for this deficiency; so that the play-room at Morning-Gleam, with its swings, hoops, cups and balls, and its baby-house furnished from kitchen to attic, was the admiration and the wonder of all the child-world in the region. Now this baby-house was densely peopled with dolls of all grades, from Victoria, with her family and maids of honor, down to a ragged-school, with its demure and self-sacrificing teachers, surrounded by their ill-conditioned pupils. All these were dressed by Maggie's own hand, and bespoke a taste, a sense of propriety, and a capability which argued well for her future usefulness as a domestic manager and an active philanthropist. But all these things were the work of the father and his child: where was the proof of a *mother's* unwearied love—the traces of her delicate taste? Ah, none so blest below but one bitter drop is mingled in the cup of joy! Many a little one who has no play-room, no baby-house, no dolls, would shrink from changing places with Maggie Bond! Her loving mother had long been an invalid, unable to bear the least confusion, and sometimes not even the light of day. Thus the poor child was obliged to play in a distant part of the house, to walk softly, and to speak in whispers, as she passed through the hall, or stole into the sick-room, night and morning, for the valued kiss from those dear white lips. Every thing in the chamber had a charm for her: the white muslin curtains trembling with the faint breeze which was suffered for a little while to breathe through their folds; the huge easy-chair with snowy dainty cover; the vases filled with her own flowers, and even the stand with its numerous bottles—all were sacred things in her eyes. The old lady who reigned supreme there, who said by solemn monosyllable or awful nod when she might and when she might not enter her domains, seemed to her innocent imagination like the regal mistress of some enchanted bower; and once she was completely overcome with amazement and gratitude when this royal dame patted her on the head, saying, "You're the quietest child I ever had to deal with in a mother's sick-room: when I get a chance to go over home, I'll give you a pin-ball my grandmother made out of a bit of the red cloak she had when she was married. She was 'most a hundred years old when she made it, and that without spectacles, too! Good-night, child."

Now this old lady, Mrs. Green, was a renowned nurse for the sick, and some thought their recovery sure if they could but secure her services. No doubt one great secret of her success was the vigilance with which she guarded her patient from all intrusion and noise. Now this very faithfulness made her the terror of all little children who had ever had a sick mother; so that when the stage brought her, with her old-fashioned hair-trunk, band-box and carpet-bag, to the front-door, they generally escaped out of the back one, avoiding the body of the house, creeping up back-stairs and playing in barns till health returned and she departed. No doubt the good woman had met with great annoyances from rude and disobedient children rushing into the room where perhaps life depended on perfect quiet, and in her zeal for the mother had lost all pity for the children. They in turn almost hated her, and dreaded her presence in their homes far more than they did the disease she came to cure.

Now Maggie Bond had heard many terrible stories about "old Mother Green," which her austere manner did not tend to dispel. But, trained to pay respect to every one about her, especially to the old, Maggie never attempted to argue any question with her, nor yet to do any thing which she saw displeased her. She sought to win her favor by saving her a few steps when in her power, and by avoiding all noise. Thus it was that she won upon the old nurse until they really became friends; so that when, after weeks of confinement, she felt that she must go home for one day and night to rest a little and see how her husband and daughter were getting along, she said to Mr. Bond, "You need not sit in the chamber every moment: you can trust Maggie to watch an hour or two any time, for she is the best child that ever lived, I do believe." When she came back she brought the promised pin-ball and a little basket full of parched corn, hazel nuts, and dried berries—"a present from Papy Green to her for being such a dear, good child." This praise, together with the honor conferred on her as nurse in Mrs. Green's absence, made poor Maggie so happy that she had to run with her treasures into her play-room to hide the tears of joy. Had some Royal Humane Society sent her a gold medal for saving a fellow-creature from death, we doubt if it could have been more highly appreciated than were these humble testimonials from such a source.

Thus you will see that, although Maggie

Bond was deprived of her mother's society, she was not always miserable, having many blessings to make up for her one great trial. During the long, sad year which followed, her affectionate father did all in his power to make her happy. He spent much of his leisure with her out of doors, lest the shadow of sickness and silence within might fall upon her young spirit and make its lasting impress there. It is no proof of love to a sick or suffering friend to sit moping in idleness and tears. Better far do we show that love by doing all in our power to relieve them and other stricken ones, and then calmly and sweetly to receive at God's hand the blessings he has left us untouched by the blight of earth. The most acceptable offering we can lay upon his altar with the prayer of faith, is a submissive spirit, resolved to do his will in the storm as well as in the sunshine. A morose, fretful, and impatient mourner cannot serve God acceptably in any way, and so did Mr. Bond feel when he strove to banish unhallowed thoughts from Maggie's mind. Together the loving pair traversed the hills, valleys, and forests in search of minerals, wild flowers, and berries; together they read their morning and evening portion of Scripture, and prayed; together they went to God's house and to the dwellings of the sick and poor. They were as the substance and the shadow; never separated save when Mr. Bond was preparing for his Sabbath services. Then Maggie studied her simple lessons for an hour or two; in which time she learned more than she would have done, hived up with a hundred weary little children, in a close, hot, school-room, in six hours. After this she was allowed to visit Nancy Darby, the one servant at the parsonage; who, having come from home with Maggie's mother when she was married, after having spent fifteen years with *her* mother, felt an interest in affairs which it is unreasonable we should expect from those poor strangers who seldom pass summer and winter in the same kitchen.

Nancy was far from being young or active, but she was faithful, capable, and full of good nature. She loved the child of the parsonage with a sincere affection, and did all she could to make up for the loss of her mother's company.

Maggie's mother was a real lady, and as such was always considerate toward her servant; never giving her an unnecessary step, nor needlessly wounding her feelings, as coarse people often do to show, they imagine, their own dignity and superiority. These delicate feelings had passed by her example to the child, and many were the little acts of kindness she performed for Nancy, thus relieving her and at the same time amusing herself. She fed the dog, the cat, and the chickens; hunted for the eggs, filled the salt-cellars, and ran little errands—all with such a cheerfulness as made it a pleasure to ask any little service at her hand.

Now to say that Nancy Darby loved Maggie, would be to give a faint idea of the ardent affection she cherished toward her. The faithful creature had never known what it was to love husband or child, being as she called herself, "a spinster;" but she did not believe that any mother's love could excel that she had for the child of Morning-Gleam. "Wern't her's," she asked, "the first hands that ever held her? Didn't she wean her, and teach her to walk and to sing? And had any person ever heard her speak a hasty word to her, whether naughty or good? And should anybody tell her that she didn't love Maggie, and that she wouldn't suffer as much for her sake as her parents would? They might *tell her so*, but she wouldn't believe it. To be sure, she had never been a mother, but she was *human* for all that, and she knew what *love* meant as woll as other folks. Did anybody think she would stay there and drudge, drudge, from day to day, with rheumatic pains in her shoulders and ancles, when she had a whole life's 'arnings laid up in the bank, if she didn't love the folks like her own flesh and blood?

Hadn't she a nephew who was well-to-do in the world, who, 'feared she might break down and make her will where she was, was teazing her fall and spring to give up hard work and live like a lady on the interest of her money, and telling her how his children would wait on her, and his wife let her have the best room for her own? And do you suppose she'd stay there if she didn't love Maggie? Why she did love her like her heart's blood, and let life or death come to the mother—nobody had better speak a harsh word to the child while Nancy Darby lived!"

CHAPTER III.

"WHY, Nancy! did you know that your best pudding-dish was broken?" exclaimed Maggie, one bright morning, as she entered the back-door with a large piece of yellow-ware in each hand. "I suppose this is Mr. Bruno's work again; and it's only a week since he broke a saucer! I'm afraid you'll get out of patience with him altogether, if he is so mischievous!"

"Bruno didn't do *that,* child," replied Nancy, without looking at Maggie, but sweeping with a vigor which bespoke a blessed forgetfulness of "the rhumaties," as she called her trouble. Her mind was evidently disturbed about something, and Maggie longed to know the cause.

"Did *you* break it, Nancy?" she ventured to ask.

Morning Gleam.

Page 30.

"Yes, child; and it's pretty lucky I broke nothing else. A dish is easily replaced, but if my heart or anybody's else is broke, it won't be so easy to get another, or to mend those we're got."

"It don't seem as if any thing *could* break your heart," said the child, gazing at the woman's huge proportions as if she saw no possible way for any outside sorrow to break through such a thick wall and smite the little inhabitants within. "Dear mother's heart might be broken with one evil word," she added, "and father's might be if he should lose *us;* and I'm sure mine would be if either of *them or you* should die; but I don't believe any thing in the world *could* break yours, Nancy—you're so strong."

Nancy threw down the broom on the painted floor with a noise which startled Maggie. She dropped into the nearest chair, drew the child upon her lap, and covering her face with her clean checked apron, burst into tears. Maggie was amazed. She had heard

Nancy scold the simple fellow who cut the wood and did the rough work; she had heard her sigh when weary or vexed at her work; but the idea that she had a fountain where she kept tears was quite new to her, and surprised her as much as it would have done had the picture of the famous Romish saint winked, or that of the Virgin shed genuine drops from the canvas, while she gazed on them.

"Why, Nancy," exclaimed Maggie, "I never knew before that you *could* cry."

"It is precious seldom, child, that I *do*, only for my sins—and that's when I'm alone with God. I haven't had such a spell since my mother died; and I'm sure *that* warn't nothin' to cry for—to see a saint go up to heaven in a chariot of fire, shoutin' 'glory' as she went! You don't remember that, do you?"

"No, Nancy, I'm sure I don't. I thought nobody but Elijah ever went up so. Did you see her go?"

"Oh, darlin' child! I don't mean that she really went up *so*. She died on her bed, and was buried like other dead folks; but she went so triumphant that it wasn't like death to me. I've never feared death since then, for I saw his sting taken away—with my own eyes I saw it. As we stood about her bed, somebody said, 'Poor mother!' but she cried out, 'Don't call me *poor:* I'm a blessed woman to-day! I wouldn't change my dyin' pillow for a throne with any queen on earth.'"

A little arm stole softly around the weeper's neck. "I hope *we* shall die so, don't you, Nancy?" whispered a soft voice. "And if we were *only sure we should,* we would never cry here. What *were* you crying for? It seems so strange to see you unhappy. I can't go to my lessons till you tell me."

"I wasn't cryin' for fear of death nor for any of my own troubles, dear: them tears was for you and yours. But," she continued, winding her large arms in a crushing embrace around Maggie, "nobody shall give you a harsh word while I live, darlin'—remember that."

A shadow passed over the sunny face of the child. "Nancy," she said in a low voice, "do you know what troubles my father this morning?"

"Troubles your father?" asked Nancy, in feigned astonishment. "He's the last one that ought to be sad to-day. He's had some beautiful letters this morning! He'll tell you by-and-by what was in them. But sittin' here babying you won't finish my work;" and springing up, she caught her broom off the floor and swept with a vigor seldom surpassed by a young kitchen-maid. "There's a bowl of milk for your kittens," she said, just as Mrs. Green entered the door with a waiter, from which her poor patient had just received her breakfast. Maggie bore the milk off to the shed, and sitting down beside the box which contained three white kittens and a Maltese sister—all too young to care for themselves—she took them into her lap and held them one at a time up to the bowl. In the meantime the nurse and Nancy Darby commenced an animated conversation, which she heard as distinctly as if addressed to herself. Nor is it at all probable her presence in the kitchen would have prevented it, neither of them being persons of very delicate perceptions or refined sensibility.

"Well, Mother Green," began Nancy, "so you're a-goin' off, are you? Well, you've got the name of bein' a hard old cretur' for help to get along with, so that girls gives notice to quit their places when they make sure you're a-comin'. So *they tell* me; but *I'll* give you a good name, if nobody else does. I could live with you all my life without one hasty word between us; more'n that, I feel grateful to you for your faithfulness to my sick folks up-stairs. Dear patient cretur'! She'll miss you, but she shan't have any less attention, for I'll see to her *myself*, if there ain't a meal got nor a dish washed in this house from Monday mornin' to Saturday night! The idea! that I could give my time up to cookin' for *company* with the name of 'nuss.' When Mr. Bond come down this mornin', and broke the news to me that his mother was comin' to spend the summer and take care of *her*, I screamed right out. 'Good patience,' says I, 'she'll die for a drink afore she'd ask such a grand old lady to run up and down-stairs for her! Why, sir,' says I, 'if your mother's a-comin' here and wants as much waitin' on as she did seven year ago, we'll need Miss Green as much as we do now; for we can put off our own folks any way. Mrs. Bond's comfort is uppermost in all our minds, and not one of us but would go a week without food or sleep if we could help her by it; that you know, sir.'"

"'That's true, Nancy,' says he, 'but you know I cannot afford to keep a nurse too; besides, my mother has mado this offer, which is a great deal for one who has no occasion to deprive herself of rest, and her feelings would surely be wounded if I forbade her doing it.' The dear soul looked as if he would sink, so I said no more; but it doesn't seem to me as if I could go through another such year as I did seven year ago no more than I could fly! If I didn't love 'em all so, I'd quit!"

"Now, Nancy," replied Mrs. Green, soothingly, "maybe you'll be disappointed as agreeable as you was with me. If you do the best you can to please her and to keep Mrs. Bond quiet too, I guess it'll all come out right: *every thing does,* if we could only believe it."

"Ah, *if* we could only believe it!" exclaimed poor Nancy, the unbidden tears beginning to flow again. "But there it is; I am the unbelievin'est cretur' in the world! It don't seem to me as if Thomas himself was any unbelieviner than I be. Now when I look back on all the way the Lord has led me, I can truly say that every trial and tribulation has been for my good. Why, it's as clear as the sun at noonday. When my father died, everybody thought my mother would have to bring up at the poor-house, with all her children, and so she thought herself. She was a good, kind mother, as far as she knowed how; but we was all comin' up like little heathens. We picked huckleberries all day Sunday, or 'tended to the sap-runnin', or something of that sort. We never went to church nor Sunday-school no more'n our poultry did. And so we was growin' up, when father got killed fellin' an oak tree. Sure enough it was a dark day; and after the funeral we was the desolatest little group ever you did see. Mrs. Bond's father was the nearest minister to us, and some of the neighbors sent for him to make a prayer afore we went to the grave. I was young, but I remember that prayer. After he'd asked God to do what nobody expected him to do for us, says he, 'Now, Lord, know I that thou hearest, and that thou wilt send answers of mercy and peace into this dwellin'.' That waren't like Thomas. Well, next day, when we was doin' up our little work with heavy hearts, who should draw up to our door but Mr. Hale, the minister, and his wife and little Rebekah—that's Mrs. Bond now. The good man got out and come in with them, and after speakin' a few comfortin' words to mother, says he, 'Now, Mrs. Darby, I come this morning to see what I can do to help you. You have a heavy charge left you, and need a friend to advise with and to assist you. Have you thought of any way by which you can bring up your family?'

"Then mother told him that the neighbors all said there was no use in tryin'—that she'd be forced to bind out the two oldest, and go with the rest on us to the poor-house; but, says she, 'I'm strong, sir, and I'll gladly work eighteen hours out of the twenty-four to feel that I wasn't a burden to nobody; and at any rate, *I mean to try!* I won't go till I see hunger starin' these children in the face. Then, rather than have them suffer, I will take the town's bounty.'

"'Now, my good woman,' says Mr. Hale, 'that's just the right spirit, and with it I don't believe you'll ever go there! If you want to put your girls out, I can provide for three of them. Two of my friends will take one apiece—they may have their choice—and Mrs. Hale will take the other.' Well, the long and the short on't is, that Pricilly went to Deacon Horne's, Susanny to the Widow Brainard's, and I, bein' a slenderish girl, and onfit for hard work, came to Mr. Hale's; a good day it was for all our souls. Pricilly, she married a decent farmer, and died leavin' a family of children that's an honor to any mother's name. Susanny died afore her time was out; but her'n was a blessed death; and here I be to-day with as little to complain on as any woman alive. Now, suppose poor father had a-lived, we might have stayed there in them pine-clearin's as ignorant as colts of the way to heaven. That was God's way to bring us all to himself. Mother, she sold her four acres of rough land and moved into the village, where she took in washin', and with our help brought up her two little ones to take care of her in her old age and feebleness. And if *I* do say it, she was an honor to the church, and Mr. Hale used to say, if anybody wants to see the power of faith, let 'em go to Widow Darby's cottage; and he said her death-bed was like the gate of heaven to many souls that stood beside it. Now don't you think I ought to believe that all things will work together for good, to them that love God?"

"I do think so, Nancy," replied Mrs. Green.

"Ah, but," said she, "the trouble is to know whether I do really love him, and whether I am one of the 'called according to his purpose.'"

"One good way to find out," added Mrs. Green, "is to search ourselves, and see whether we are willing to submit to God's will in all things."

"Yes, yes!" said Nancy, "*in all things!* Now in some things I'm the submissivest cretur' ever you see. When mother died, I give her to God with a cheerful, thankful heart, though she was the dearest thing I had on earth. I felt, when I saw that her spirit was gone, to cry out, 'What am I that God should bless and honor me by giving my best friend a place at his right hand, where are pleasures forevermore?' And when I made her ready for the grave with my own hands, and helped lay her to rest in her coffin, I felt nearer to heaven than I ever did before. It did seem to me as if Jesus stood there beside us; and that I still had hold of mother's hand, though she had stepped in through the gate and I was still outside. It was so easy to give up my will to God's will then!"

"It is often easier to bear great trials than little ones," remarked Mrs. Green, timidly, for she evidently felt during this conversation that Nancy Darby was no common kitchen-drudge.

"Well, then," continued the speaker, "you remember when the 'Green Valley Savin's Bank' broke I had two years' hard earnings in it laid up against old age. When somebody come in and told me I had lost it, says I, 'I'm glad it's *that* instead of my hope of heaven; and from that day to this, that two hundred dollars has never cost me a tear nor an hour's sleep. I just said in my heart, 'God saw I would be better without it,' and that was an end of it! But it does seem as if this thing now is more than I could bear: to have real particular company here orderin' what they'd like to eat, and comparin' every thing with what they have 'at my daughter Caroline's,' and at the same time to feel the whole care of that dear sufferer up-stairs on my mind! If you was to stay I wouldn't care so much, for you'd see that all was quiet up-stairs; but I guess we'll have nurses enough up-stairs when my lady takes your place. She kept young Mrs. Bond's cheeks red pretty much the whole year she spent here afore, with her hard hints and smart speeches."

"I've heard that she was a pretty stern old lady," replied Mrs. Green; "but they say she's very religious, and good to the poor, so I guess you'll get along with her. It is always easier for me to bear with the ugly ways of good folks than with those of wicked people; for I know they *mean* to do right."

"Oh, well, then, it's a good deal *harder* for me; for I think they've no excuse for bein' ugly after they've learned the spirit of Jesus; but these poor cretur's that's yet in their sins, oh, how much I can bear with them afore I lose my patience! I feel to cry, 'Father, forgive 'em, for they know not what they do!' There's old Mose Sawyer that cuts our wood: he stutters so a body can't get a straight answer from him, except when he *swears*, and then he rolls out his words as clear as you can your'n. It goes right to my heart when I hear him revile the name of my Master; but pity for his soul is above every other feelin'. But if it was a man who knew more, or who had had good examples from his youth up, I do fully believe that I should want to strike off his right ear, as that spirited disciple did the High Priest's servant's. But in this case, a fine lady, with learnin', and religion, and gentility, and money, comes here, and because *we* don't believe just as she wants us to, thinks she's goin' to rule us with a rod of iron, and forms all her speeches just to hurt our feelin's."

"Why, she's very pious, isn't she?" asked Mrs. Green. "I don't see how she and your folks can help agreein'. I'm sure she cannot find any fault with them."

"She's pious—I believe in my very heart she is; but her's ain't the softenin', meltin' kind of religion. It's the kind that would smite off the right ear of sinners, and call down lightnin' from heaven on 'em. And yet I do believe she's a sincere lover of the Lord, and hater of sin. When she persecutes, it's for conscience-sake, and that's what makes it so hard. You can't reason with her no more than you can with that stone wall."

"I wouldn't try," replied Mrs. Green. "I hold on to my belief, and let her alone in her's."

"I guess you wouldn't hold your own long

in peace if she had any rule over you. She'd put her iron heel on to your conscience, and she wouldn't stop grindin' you till every speck of Methodism was ground out o' *you*. She would never let you say 'John Wesley,' as long as you lived, again!"

"Why," exclaimed Mrs. Green, in an energetic voice, and dilating her eyes to their utmost capacity, "don't she like Methodists?"

"No, indeed," replied Nancy, "she don't nor us Baptists, nor other heretics. Her own Church is infallible, and she'll never forgive our folks—the Hales—for proselyting her only son. She says she's always felt guilty that she didn't go to college with him and watch him all the time, to see what books he read and what company he kept; then she might have *saved him* from bein' led astray! The idea of bein' led astray by our folks!"

"Then she and the Hales ain't of the same religion?" asked Mrs. Green.

"Yes, they be; for I will have it that it is the same faith. Her Lord and her Saviour is ours; but because we dare to differ from her on some points, she talks about 'her religion' and 'our religion.' Look at the pastor of her own church and yours and Mr. Bond: don't they stand shoulder to shoulder against Unitarianism, and every other error here, like a band of brethren? But she must set up that we've started a new religion to break down the one that the Pilgrim Fathers bled and died for."

"Oh, well, we're all poor, inconsistent mortals, if we're left to ourselves," said Mrs. Green. "If she's hard, Nancy, you must just try to show her that you're tender and merciful and forbearing. It takes two to make a quarrel, and don't you be one of them here. I believe one reason people—I mean girls in kitchens—think me such a tyrant is, that I won't dispute with them. I lay down my rules about the sick-room, and then, no matter how much they fuss or fret, I say no more, but move right on like a deaf and dumb woman. In the end, however, they learn who their friend is; for many that have said every thing against me have come to me for a home in sickness, or when they were out of a place. I've learned that a quiet perseverance in the way of duty is the safest and easiest way to get along."

"That's all very true; but when duty looks two ways, what is a poor woman to do? It is certainly my duty to see that dear sufferer up-stairs attended to, lifted night and mornin', as you do, watched over and 'tended, encouraged and cheered up, strengthened with little delicacies, and kept quiet; and *maybe* it's my duty to stay down-stairs to make nice pastry and cook rich food—such as we can't afford—for company that pretends to be *nuss*, while I do the work. And, at the same time, it's my duty to hear every thing said against my faith and hold my tongue, thus seeming to thank her for condescendin' to despise us! I tell you, Mrs. Green, it isn't always so easy to know what duty is. But I do think a girl that has lived with mother and daughter twenty-five years (though rapidly verging toward forty, Nancy always called herself *a girl*), might have a little right to speak in a house; and speak I will! I'll tell Mr. Bond that if he'll get an Irish girl to do the drudgery, I'll try to keep house and be nurse and waiter for the old lady. And if he don't, I guess I'll go a while to my nephew's, where I shan't see nor hear any of the trouble."

"Well, you must do as you think best; but I will warn you all," replied Mrs. Green, "that a little worriment of mind may upset all I have done for Mrs. Bond in all these weeks. If she isn't kept still and her mind easy, she'll die: that's as sure as she's alive now! But I'm afraid Mr. Bond will think my resting-time is long this morning: though he's never weary of sitting beside that bed—the dear, kind man."

CHAPTER IV.

MAGGIE had listened with good attention to the foregoing conversation, although a great portion of it was quite unintelligible to her mind. All the impression she gained was that Grandma Bond was a very different lady from Grandma Hale; and that Nancy did not like fine ladies, and was not willing to wait upon them. There was a vague feeling clinging to her mind when she went to her books and her play, that the expected visitor did not love "Mamma" as everybody else did, and that she was coming to take care of her only from a sense of duty. But this idea was so much out of the way that she soon shook it off, and began picturing to her mind the elegant stranger. Their neighbor, Captain Blount, had recently taken his plain, motherly companion to Havre, and brought her back again quite a new being; an elegant and magnificent lady she seemed in the eyes of the child who was so much a stranger to fashion. The plainly-dressed, silver-streaked hair which went to France, came home curled, glossy, and black; the faded brown cheeks had in some mysterious way stolen the bloom from Parisian roses; while the black silk dress and gray bonnet had given place to a plume-laden pink hat, and a gaudy brocade robe, flounced from top to bottom. Good-natured Mrs. Blount, in undergoing this mighty transformation herself, had not forgotten the village children at home; in lieu of the oranges, nuts, and raisins they used to receive from her capacious store-room, they were now favored with red scarfs, tinsel combs, embroidered aprons, and the like.

Now when Maggie heard her aged relative accused of being "a fine lady," she at once set her down as a counterpart of Mrs. Blount, whose appearance on her return had given great offence to Nancy Darby, who fully agreed with St. Paul in his view of the dress to be worn by women professing godliness. Although so young and so fully impressed with Nancy's importance and good sense, Maggie had yet discernment enough to know that she was not the standard of good taste, and to see the differences in her purchases and those of her mother; she therefore made great allowance for Nancy's severity toward "fine ladies," and grew quite impatient to hear from her father when she might look for her grandmother's arrival.

"My daughter," said Mr. Bond, as he closed the book after her simple recitations were over, "did you know I had just received a letter from your Aunt Caroline?"

"No, indeed, papa," cried Maggie, in an ecstacy of delight. "Do please to read it aloud to me."

"Aunt Caroline," or "Mrs. Percy," as strangers called her, was the only sister of Mr. Bond. She was the wife of a prosperous merchant in a distant city, and being, save

Maggie's father, her mother's only child, claimed that her house was the proper house for the old lady. She had a large, fine mansion, several servants, and no children; and being one of those light-hearted, whole-souled creatures with whom we meet, though rarely, she chose, out of consideration to the limited means of her brother, and his wife's delicate health, to insist on "keeping mother." She had *kept* her as long as in her power, and until all her golden chains had turned, in the old lady's eyes, to rusty iron bars; her silken meshes to rough, hempen nets. "She had *resolved* to go to Massachusetts to take care of Rebekah, and written to announce her intention!" Aunt Caroline's letter followed hers by the next mail, coming like a sunbeam after a cloud; for, much as the pastor loved his widowed mother, there was to him a restraint and a rebuke in her very presence; and just now, of all times, he loved the peace and joy of heaven to brood over his silent dwelling. The drooping flower of his heart seemed only able to live in the sunshine of smiles and gentle words; and however strong he might be to brave the storm of religious controversy above, or the wind of domestic contention below-stairs, he knew it would at once lay *her* low. He now called to his aid that faith in God which he was ever holding out to his people as a sure refuge in every trial. He read Aunt Caroline's joyous epistle to Maggie with its promises of "pretty things to be sent in grandma's trunk;" and hints about some mysterious present which that dear old lady was then engaged in sealing up with red wax for the same little girl, and begging her darling little niece to remember that when people grew old they could not bear with the noise and questions of little children, as when younger and stronger. She hinted, too, that it would not be well for her mother to be shut up too long in the sick-room, and that Maggie would be doing a good work by taking her among the poor and sick in the village as much as possible; and closed by saying that for the sake of all she loved at Morning-Gleam and those bound thither, she had one request to make—that kind, faithful Nancy Darby might take upon her broad shoulders and her affectionate heart all the burdens of the sick-room, while *her* own purse should supply wages for a kitchen-maid such as Nancy herself might choose. Nancy laughed until she wept tears of gratitude when this letter was read in the kitchen for her especial benefit. "Well, dear me," she exclaimed, "that Miss Caroline always was the beautifulest cretur' that ever lived; she sees all her trials turned into mercies at once—she finds a jewel in every toad's head! Mrs. Green said it would all come out right, and so it has: *almost* before I prayed I've got my answer. All I asked was that I might have the privilege of spendin' and bein' spent in that sick-room, and my request is granted. When you answer that letter, sir, please to send a thousand thanks to Mrs. Percy, and tell her Nancy understands matters, and will do just what *she* wants done here."

Had any stranger seen the humble creature, after this morning, joyfully at her work, and listened to her triumphant songs of praise and gratitude, he would have been more likely to think her just fallen heir to a fortune, rather than to a new heritage of toil by day and of watching by night. The labor and responsibility which would have crushed a less unselfish woman to the earth, were received as tokens of God's favor by this lowly, loving creature. Thus often are God's dealings with us mercies or chastisements, according to the spirit in which we receive them.

The day of Grandma Bond's arrival has come, and while her son and little Maggie are listening for wheels, and watching for carriages laden with big trunks, little trunk, band-box, bundle, we will give our dear, patient reader a little insight into the character of the expected guest, with some account of her antecedents. She had descended in a straight line from a brave, rigid, old Puritan, who came over in the May-Flower, and from him had inherited a strong love of religious liberty—that is, according to her interpretation, liberty to worship God as her own conscience directed, and to force other people to worship as *she did.* It was her honest boast that she was descended from two early Puritans—one, a celebrated divine, and the other, a ruling-elder in that pure church; and that from that day which tried the souls of her godly ancestors, not one of the long line on either side had ever swerved from the most rigid form of the faith they braved the sea to plant, till (and with shamefacedness and great humbling of soul she would confess it), till her own, only, and beloved son, Henry Endicott Cotton Bond, had proved recreant! She mourned and lamented this sad defection of him who was at once the joy and the grief of her life. "Little," she said, "did she think when, with a widow's heart, she devoted herself to those children, teaching them to follow the footsteps of those holy men, that one of them would ever be classed among deserters, who turn the world up-side down! She had expected to see this son, elegant in person, refined in manners, and sound in learning, fill some old pulpit hallowed by the preaching of John Cotton or Thomas Hooker. But what *was* he? A plain pastor of a village Baptist church —good and pious, it is true, but who, had he lived in those early days which had such a glory in her eyes, might have been fined, had his tongue bored, or been whipped on Boston Common! The history of those times was as familiar to her mind as that of the Creation to every Sunday-school child, and was a never-failing source of thought and conversation; for, beside her unbroken line of ancestry, which she saw with miraculous vision untainted by heresy, there was a real soul-bond between herself and those who clipped off Quakers' ears, bored their tongues with red-hot irons, and also whipped, fined, and imprisoned the Baptists. She had but one only fault to find with these early lights of the New England Churches: their plans and purposes were good, but they did not carry them out to the full extent they might have done with the sole power in their hands. Had they hung Roger Williams, whipped out the little spark of life they left in Obediah Holmes, and inflicted on John Clark what Gov. Endicott in his charge told him he deserved—death, she might this day have been a proud and happy woman! She did not approve of harsh measures for their own sake; nor yet was she a woman of blood. On the contrary, she was exceedingly merciful—in her way. In worldly sorrows she was tender and sympathizing, ever imparting of her substance to clothe and feed the poor; ever ready to sacrifice ease and rest for the sick and suffering. It was only when it came to matters of *religion* that she was hard, uncharitable, and tyrannical. She called it "merciful to crush out the spirit of error which, if suffered to live, would be the death of souls: just as a compassionate physician cuts out the cancer to save the life of his patient." She would "do any thing for the *bodies* of Roman Catholics even; but she firmly believed it was the duty of our government to burn down their churches, banish their priests, and force the common people to attend Protestant church and Sunday-school! Were they not the enemies of God? Surely it was our province to make them his friends, to break their chains of superstition, so that they might enjoy as well as ourselves *liberty of conscience*—that inestimable blessing."

"Hark, Maggie! There's a carriage heavily laden with trunks, and the driver is trying to make out the house. Let us go down, and if it is grandma, meet her at the gate."

Mr. Bond soon knew the huge initials on the trunks, and waved his white handkerchief to the driver to stop. With his own hands he opened the door, let down the steps, and almost lifted the weary traveler from the coach. As she leaned upon his arm while going up the gravel-walk, poor Maggie, who had not yet attracted her notice, stepped around the other side and a little before her, so as to get a glance into the face of the "fine lady," whom she now thought traveling in the disguise of a plain, ordinary person. At length she ventured to touch her hand, as much as to say, "Here is little Maggie;" but a cold glance, and an exclamation, "Oh, Endicott, how much that child resembles the Hales!" with "There, you may carry my reticule in, child," were the only tokens she received that she was seen at all.

They entered the hall of Morning-Gleam cottage, the numerous trunks followed, and the door closed behind them. The shadows were beginning to fall, and lamps had not as yet been lighted. Madam Bond, as we must now call the guest, heaved a deep, deep sigh—one which seemed to come up from the lowest corners of the heart.

"Are you sick or only tired, grandma, dear?" asked the affectionate little girl, all unused as she was to such doleful sounds.

"Neither, child," replied the old lady, without looking in her face, but sinking into a rocking-chair, as she entered the sitting-room. "Morning-Gleam is a strange name for this place: Night-Shade would be more appropriate. Here, put away this shawl and umbrella, Experience." Maggie took the two named articles, and then stood waiting as if for a third.

"There, go, child, and don't stand looking in my face," cried the new-comer with genuine energy in her tone.

"Wasn't there one other thing you wanted me to put away, grandma?" asked Maggie, timidly.

"No, child; only umbrella and shawl."

"I thought there were *three* things."

Mr. Bond smiled. He saw that Maggie was waiting for something answering to the name "Experience." She had hardly passed from the room when she heard a call after her.

"Margaret Experience! Come back here,

child!" Maggie halted, entered the room, and stood overwhelmed with confusion. "Margaret Experience, will you tell your woman I want tea hastened as much as possible?" The old lady's eyes were fixed on the child, and she was evidently addressing her; but what did she mean? Maggie now remembered Nancy's tears about her grandmother's coming, and began to wonder if the old lady were not crazy. Tears started to her eyes, and she would fain have thrown herself into her father's arms, but could not do so without passing by grandma, who might catch her for aught she could tell!

"Endicott!" cried Madam Bond, "why does that child stand staring at me so? Why don't she put away my things and carry my orders to the kitchen?"

"Mother," said Mr. Bond, "she don't know who you are talking to—we always call her Maggie! Run my love," he said to the child, "and ask Nancy to hasten tea a little."

"Why, Endicott!" said the old lady reproachfully, "I always thought you named that child for *me!*"

"We did, mother; but we don't call her by the whole of it at once—it is too long," replied the son, trying to suppress a smile.

"I don't believe the child knows what her name is," answered Madam Bond, tartly. A little step was now heard moving timidly through the hall, as if doubtful whether or not to risk an entrance.

"Experience!" shouted she, "Experience! Come here!"

This harmless word became suddenly a tone of terror to poor Maggie. "Open Sesame," had not more magic power on the door of the robbers' cave than "Experience" on her ear. The little feet beat a swift retreat, nor did Maggie stop till she found safety in the strong arms of Nancy Darby.

"Either that child is an idiot, or she don't know her own name!" exclaimed Grandma Bond with a sigh, the usual accompaniment of her sayings.

"She's a shy little fawn," said her father. "I'll catch her and bring her back."

"Don't bring her to me against her will, I beg you," exclaimed the old lady. "I never take children captive."

Maggie was soon led in with a forced smile on her lips, and took her stand by her grandmother's chair quite of her own will. She had received her father's word that their guest was in her right mind and harmless; and that was enough.

"What's your name, child?" was the first question put to her.

"Maggie Bond," replied she.

"Maggie's no name at all! What's written in your books and upon your clothes?"

"Maggie Bond."

"Is that possible, Endicott?" asked the old lady, looking reproachfully at her son.

"Oh, mother dear, we are most informal people here," said the gentleman, "but we do write her name 'Maggie E. B. Bond.' Isn't it so on your silver cup and spoon and fork and napkin-ring, dear?"

"Yes, sir," replied the child. "M. E. B. B."

"What does that 'E. B.' stand for?" asked Madam Bond.

"*B* for Brewster," answered Maggie. "I'm named for *you*, grandma, and when you were a little girl, ma says your name was 'Maggie Brewster.'"

"*Maggie* is no name at all. My maiden name was 'Margaret Experience Brewster; and that's your's if you're my namesake."

Maggie hung her head at the thought of this new appendage; especially as henceforth it would always recall the strange tone and manner which so alarmed her on hearing it.

"It is a very long name for so little a girl, mother, and we thought we should leave out the 'E.,'" said Mr. Bond, who, undutiful son that he was, had taken the liberty to drop one or two of his own names.

Madam Bond sighed. "I suppose," she said, "you are aware, Endicott, that such changes in a name might affect the child very seriously in a court of law. For instance, if, in case of your's and Caroline's death, I should leave her my estate, my nieces, the Downs' girls, could easily break the will by forcing her to prove that she was *the* 'Margaret Experience Brewster Bond' mentioned in the parish register and in the will."

"I don't know how it may be in the *will*, but her name is not recorded in any parish record," said the father.

"Very true—poor thing!" sighed grandma. "No vows were ever registered for her; no obligations ever entered into to bring her up in the nurture and admonition of the Lord!"

"No, not *publicly*, mother; but whatever may be said of me, Maggie is the child of a praying woman, who has given her to the Lord in faith and love. But here comes

Nancy to welcome you and to call us to tea."

It was against the principle of Nancy to flatter or to speak one unmeaning word of welcome. She did not say, "I'm glad to see you;" but only, "I hope you are well, Mrs. Bond," and, "I'm afraid you're weary;" to which Madam only replied, "I am quite well, and not at all weary." And then they took their seats at a table which would have done honor to any housekeeper in the land; while Nancy sat beside the sick-bed, and left her new help—Kitty Flynn—to play waiting-maid. Grandma announced her intention of waiting till morning to see the invalid, and retired early to rest, although "not at all weary," after a journey of six hundred miles. So resolutely determined was this old lady not to grow old nor to die until her hour came, that she would never admit that she felt the weakness or infirmities of which even school-girls are so ready to complain. She has gone to her pillow: may the angels of mercy and gentleness watch her slumbers, fanning her brow and touching her heart the while with their soft, white wings!

Maggie's ideas of fine ladies were wonderfully confused as she laid her head down that night. Grandma, tall, gaunt, stately, and plainly robed, was the very opposite of Mrs. Blount; "but perhaps," she thought, "when the trunks were opened the showy garments, and her own presents, of which not a word had as yet been said, might appear together. And wondering what these presents could be —particularly the one sealed up so carefully in red wax—she slipped off to the land of dreams; there to see her name written all over her beautiful books, "Experience Bond," and to hear the rude village-boys around the tavern and market shout after her as she went to the Post-office, "Experience Bond!" and to take with childish delight from her father's box a gilded letter from Aunt Caroline, directed to "Margaret Experience Brewster Bond." But the night, with its imaginary troubles, passed away, and the dear child awoke in the morning grateful for all her mercies, among which was considered as not least that she was still herself—father's dear little Maggie Bond.

CHAPTER V.

MORNING came to the cottage with blessings on its wings. It brought hope to the pastor, sleep to the sufferer, joy to the child, a magic anodyne to grandma's chafed spirit, patience to Nancy Darby, and a good breakfast—than which no boon could be more welcome—to the new servant, Kitty Flynn. Every one seemed resolved to be cheerful and content; so that when Madam Bond ordered her trunks to be carried up-stairs, Nancy called Kitty to the work, albeit she would have chosen that the command had taken the form of a request. She rejoiced at the prospect of the trunks being opened at any sacrifice of feeling to herself; as Maggie, child that she was, knowing that they contained her hidden treasures, kept gazing at them, in the same spirit that the merchant looks through his telescope at the quarantined vessel laden with his, as yet, unseen riches; or as the student with his longing eyes feasts upon the books which are yet to unfold to him stories of mysterious lore. But to the amazement of Nancy, "big trunks, little trunks, band-box, bundle," were all packed away in a dark closet at the end of the hall, to be opened, their owner said, "After a few days, when she should feel like it."

"If I may make so bold, madam," said Nancy, "I would like to ask one favor; that is, that you would take out Maggie's presents *now*, as the poor child is all impatience to see them. When I put her to bed last night she made me *guess* for ten minutes what they were, and then *she* guessed. You know children are children, and we were all children once, ma'am."

Madam Bond turned her cold, gray eyes on the presuming speaker, and asked in great surprise, "What presents are you talking about? Who said I had brought her any thing?"

"Her aunt, Mrs. Percy, wrote about them, and her poor little heart can't wait any longer," answered Nancy, nothing daunted.

"When did Mrs. Percy write that, I should like to know?" exclaimed the old lady.

"Well, I guess her letter came by the same mail or the very next one after your'n," replied Nancy. "At any rate, I heard 'em both read at once."

"*You* heard them read, did you? Well, Mrs. Percy never mentioned to *me* that she was writing. I told her *I* would let them know my own plans." Nancy was silent; she feared to go any farther, seeing that she had already strayed on to forbidden ground. "But as to the presents for Margaret—if there are any, for I've not told her so—she must wait my pleasure for them. I'm sorry to see such an avaricious disposition in the child. It will be a good discipline for her to wait; it will teach her patience. She's wonderfully like the Hales—body and mind! Don't you see it yourself, Nancy?"

7

"To be sure I do, ma'am; and that's one reason she is so dear to my heart. Them Hales is dear, lovely, Christian people, and it does seem hard to have them so far away from us. But their letters are like good news from a far country; and by-and-by we'll all be together again. That'll be a blessed day for our dear Mrs. Bond, she does love her people so! What a comfort it would be to us all if they were only as near as they used to be afore they went West."

"Umph!" sighed Madam Bond, as she turned the key upon her trunks and Maggie's hopes. "If you think Mrs. Bond is ready to see me, Nancy, I'll go into her room now."

'You can go in, but, remember," said Nancy, "the doctor says *life depends on quiet!* Her disease is in the heart, so we must all look out how we meddle with her heart."

Madam deigned no reply to the faithful nurse, but obeyed her orders to the very letter, from a stern sense of duty. Had she believed it binding upon her to sit by the bed till death released her, she would have done it; and not one of the Brothers of Silence from the Convent of Pisa could have kept his vow with more faithfulness than did she her resolution in no way to annoy or disturb the sick one, to minister to whose comfort she had come. Hers was no soft woman's heart to melt at the sight of suffering; but rather a battering engine to drive it away. With the spirit of Peter the Hermit, she might, had she lived in the time of the Crusaders, have led an army successfully to the rescue of the Saviour's tomb from the hands of the Infidels. It seemed indeed a sad waste of noble energy that she could do nothing of the sort in the times on which she had fallen; for she was as one born out of due season. She had the soul for any fate: she could fight, labor, endure any thing but *yield*. That word was not in all her vocabulary; and so fearful was she lest she might some day be called to such a trial that she avoided looking any subject in the face on which she had once expressed an opinion. Had she been, like Cranmer, called to go to the stake for her faith, she could have done it with a firm tread and head erect; but never like him recanted and then held up the treacherous hand, publicly confessing that with that he had sinned, and begging that that might be first consumed. She looked upon death as an inevitable law of nature; and considered it rebellion against High Heaven to mourn the lost. She could say with truth that her lovely first-born babe had been *given to God*, not torn from her embrace by death as a ruthless tyrant; that her own hands had laid it in the coffin, rejoicing

> "That aught so pure, so beautiful, was hers
> To bring before her God."

And when the noble partner of her life was stricken down by her side, she quailed not, neither did her faith fail her; but, pale, stern, and enduring, she sailed on through life's cold waters with her children, like a majestic iceberg decked with unnipped blossoms. She was a noble woman with one great lack in her character—who of us has less?—that one element, undefinable, which makes woman what she is as wife and mother, sister and friend. She would have made a splendid Lady Abbess had she been a Roman Catholic, a Maria Theresa had she been a Queen; but being neither, she had done much good in the world by her firm principles and resolute, untiring action. With all her lack of tenderness and womanly grace of heart and manner, let us do her full justice by saying that the world would be a better, a holier, a happier place were there more in it like her. Could such energy as hers have been diffused among her gentler, lovelier sisters, what might not woman accomplish in that cause so dear to the Christian heart, in which, since she stood in all her meekness and sorrow beside the cross and the sepulchre, she has been so important a laborer.

Now, icebergs melt when they float through sunny waters, and stones are worn away beneath a continual dropping. It was impossible to dwell in the atmosphere of Morning-Gleam without feeling its softening influence; especially now that even Nancy Darby had resolved to bear and forbear, to yield every personal feeling for Mrs. Bond's sake, and what she couldn't do for hers to do for Christ's sake. Things moved on so smoothly that the humble woman declared she could never doubt again that all things work for good. Madam was permitted to carry the keys, to deal out the medicine, and to have a general supervision over the sick-room, while the labor fell on others. Thus she was allowed to feel that her coming was not in vain, while Mrs. Bond was favored with the more congenial nursing of Nancy, and the old lady spared time to visit with little "Margaret," as she insisted on calling the child, the poor and the sick of the village. Her gifts to these were never of the delicate kind, such as flowers, birds, jellies, and syllabub, but of the more substantial sort, as soup, beef, red flannel, and coal.

Among these sufferers she found one most congenial spirit—old Betsy Simpson—a pauper, or rather a pensioner on the bounty of her brethren—both lame and blind. So inured had she become to suffering and privation that it seemed to her as her rightful heritage; and her strong will enabled her to *endure*, while her firm, noble faith saw blessings where others could discern only afflictions. Nurtured by the bitter draughts her great Physician had seen best to administer, she grew in grace and became strong in the Lord and in the power of his might; while many around her, fed upon the finest of the wheat and nourished upon strengthening cordials, grew weakly, sickened, and perished by the way before they even caught sight of the promised land. The conversation of these two strong-minded women was not without its effect on the tender heart of Maggie, who was ever a patient listener. There were points in which they were unlike: one could *endure* tribulation, the other *rejoice* in it; one could *do* a favor but never *receive* one, the other could gratefully accept, without the power or the prospect of returning all which Providence sent in her way. The one was *born* in a certain church (so she said), *therefore* that church must be founded on a rock, and its smallest tenet immutable; the other was "born in sin," and, when brought to God, without any predilections or prejudices for or against any particular creeds, had searched the Scriptures with all simplicity of mind to ascertain the will of God, neither daring nor desiring to add to or to take from the inspired standard of truth. There were, therefore, as we may well suppose, some decided points of difference between these two women. Still their Christian experience was in a good degree the same; and upon it they both loved to dwell.

"Ah, yes," sighed out Madam Bond, as she sat in the poor apartment of Betsy Simpson, "we have both been led through thorny paths, through floods and flames, and the only wonder is that we are here to-day in the land of the living! We both have one mercy left—we are out of hell!"

"Oh," cried Betsy, "we each have ten thousand mercies; every breath we draw is a blessing from our Father's hand, and I can truly say, to the praise of His grace, that poor and blind and maimed though I am, I enjoy life far more than scores who have plenty, and the health and senses to enjoy it."

"Our afflictions have been of a very different nature; for I suppose God deals out to his rebellious children just that discipline which he sees best calculated to humble them," replied Madam Bond. "I don't think there are many women who could bear better than myself the death of their friends; and I do believe, had I been called to drink the cup of poverty or endure bodily pain, I could have done either with a martyr's spirit! And I often think such would have been better discipline for *me*, than the galling mortifications which have been laid upon me."

Betsy turned her sightless balls toward the speaker, and her lips parted as if she were about to ask what had befallen her that had brought such disgrace; but probably the supposition that she had ruined sons—one in prison, and another, perhaps, sentenced to be hung—may have checked her question. She simply said, "Well, every heart knoweth its own bitterness, and the stranger intermeddleth not with its joys."

"I've had few *joys*, that any one would want to meddle with," said Madam Bond, mournfully shaking her head and sighing; "and, as I said before, I really think that crushing trouble would have been better for me, and I'm sure easier to bear, than the grinding mortifications which chafe without probing the proud spirit."

"You may have thought, ma'am, that Abana and Pharpar, rivers of your own selection, were quite as cleansing as the waters of Jordan, of God's own choosing. But we must yield to him, and receive our cleansing where he appoints. He won't consult our pride and vainglory when he deigns to heal us. I don't know what your trials have been, but I doubt not you will praise God for *just what he has sent* when we get home."

Madam Bond, heaving a sigh which might have drawn sympathy from a stone, exclaimed, "My chief sorrow has come through my children—disappointment in all my hopes of them! Now, whether this is for a judgment on my laxness in early discipline, or whether it is that chastening which for the present is not joyous but grievous, I know not."

"Ah, poor, dear woman!" exclaimed Betsy, in a tone of the tenderest sympathy, "my heart aches for you! But God is able to bring them back to the paths of virtue. I never knew before that you had any other children but our minister and Mrs. Percy, both of whom are an honor to you."

"They *are all* I have," replied madam, in her calm, cold voice; "and, as the world judges,

I might be proud of them. But it is a sore trial for one of my temperament to feel herself forsaken of her children in her old age."

Poor Betsy could not read the countenance of her visitor, and as she well knew that she lived with Mrs. Percy, she couldn't understand in what sense she was forsaken; so she kept silence.

"My son, your pastor, Betsy, is a truly good man; but he has forsaken the church of his fathers—the first of a long line from the Pilgrims to do so—turned a deaf ear to all his widowed mother's entreaties, set at naught all my baptismal vows for him, and scorned his consecration in infancy. Mind, Betsy, my good woman, I am saying nothing against your church—indeed, I believe there are good, well-meaning people amongst them; but it is against my own son for leaving the faith in which he was born, and trying to pull down that which his forefathers built up with sacrifice and toil."

A quiet smile passed over the face of the

blind woman as she said, "Well, Mrs. Bond, we must leave these matters of conscience for each to judge of for himself. We must all answer to God for the use of the light he has given us."

"It was no matter of *conscience* with my son," replied Madam Bond, a little nettled. "While in college he fell desperately in love with old father Hale's daughter; and while his head was half turned with romantic nonsense, the family, through Rebekah—a lovely Christian and a very charming woman—inveigled him into their church!"

Betsy evidently understood her visitor too well to enter into any argument, so she only replied in a soothing tone, "You still have Mrs. Percy with you."

"Yes, *in name*," replied madam, sighing. "But she is more than half Baptist; and were I in my grave to-morrow might be a whole one. She has great charity for all, and cannot sympathize at all in my decided views. And as to my dear son, he is now as obstinate in his belief as if a voice from heaven had proclaimed in his ear, 'This is the way: walk ye in it!' I never could see where he got that stern resolution: he surely did not inherit it from his father, for he was a man of the loveliest temperament, and ever ready to yield—save where conscience was involved! *Obstinate* he never was. But my lot is as it is; and I have only to submit to it, and endure with as much patience as I can command."

Notwithstanding she saw the perfect absurdity of Madam Bond's ideas of trial, poor, innocent Betsy really pitied her; for she had learned by experience that our lot is often one of joy or sorrow according to the medium through which we view it. She, the poor, the feeble, the friendless, the blind, the maimed, actually pitied the lady of means, of health, and vigor, surrounded with friends and cherished by affectionate children. Gladly, had it been in her power, would she have shared with her the sweet spirit of content our Father had sent to sweeten her otherwise bitter cup.

But she could not: it was a heritage which she had not power to communicate, and one she would not have exchanged for worlds. Ah, there is many a king, many a priest unto God, many a princess, in the cheerless walls of an almshouse; but are these therefore *poor?* Nay, they may in reality be the rich ones of the region; those who, could all be laid open, would be the envied of their neighbors? Betsy Simpson carried about with her from day to day the dignity of a king's daughter, although the purple and the fine linen were not hers now, but were reserved for another and a rapidly approaching day. She coveted no man's gold or silver, but rejoiced in her own lot—the necessaries of life now, and, beyond, an inheritance in light, undefiled, never to pass away.

CHAPTER VI.

AS the days wore away, Maggie became well assured in her own mind that one, at least, of grandma's trunks must have been removed from the dark hiding-place and opened; for one dress after another—satin, silk, or crape, though all of the same sombre hue and puritanical cut; shawl, mantilla, and cardinal; caps trimmed with black, white or purple—appeared as occasion required. Nancy Darby "felt sure that all them was never packed in her *ridicule*, and the stern old lady was trying, in a most tantalizing manner, the patience of our dear child, and showing that she meant not to give up the package Aunt Caroline had sent until first teazed for it; when she would say in triumph, 'Oh, how much that child is like the Hales!'" So the loving creature gave the little one she loved a lesson on the subject.

"Maggie, my dear," she said, one day, "I'm as sure as I want to be that them trunks have been opened, and that madam is expecting every day that you'll ask for your Aunt Caroline's present. But don't you do it, dear —on no account, don't! For everybody loves patient children, and your grandmother will think ten times more of you if you can live as long without them as she can with them. Now be a good, obedient child, and never let her know you remember any thing about her promise, and then next time I go to Boston I'll buy you 'The babes in the wood' and 'Cinderella, or the glass slippers'—two beautiful books we used to have when we were children and lived in the pine clearin's back of the town where your Grandfather Hale spent his life afore he went out West to end his days with your Uncle John—the dear, blessed old man. Oh, how beautiful your mother used to wait for things when she was little! She never teazed, nor worried, nor fretted, and everybody on earth loved Rebekah Hale! I guess they did love her, and they'll all love you too if you're like her."

Now Maggie Bond, with all that was silly and childish about her, was remarkable for some traits which would be an ornament to any person. She, like her grandmother, had a great deal of resolute endurance; and having been trained to the most implicit obedience from her earliest days, it had become as second nature for her to yield her own will to that of her superiors.

"I'm very glad you told me not to ask for my presents, Nancy," replied the child, "for I was just thinking I would this afternoon, as maybe grandma had forgotten them."

"Forgotten them? No, no, child! It's only sick folks or weak-minded ones that *forget*. She never does, nor do any such wise ones."

"I don't forget, either, do I?" cried Maggie, her eyes brightening at this new evidence of her own wisdom.

"No, no," answered Nancy. "You've got

a great deal of your grandmother's blood in you; and," she added in an undertone, as if speaking to herself, "I guess she'll find it out before she goes home. I've heard that people's looks and ways oftener show themselves in the second than in the third generation after them. I guess she'll see that there's some *Brewster* in folks as well as Hale! Now you remember, dear, to do just right about this, and when your presents come, they'll look all the handsomer to you than if you'd got 'em the first night. Why, think on't: if you'd had 'em right off, you wouldn't care half as much about them to-day! If 'twas candy, 'twould have all been eat up 'fore now; if books, you'd have read 'em all through; and if toys, we should all have admired them and they'd be an old story, like them Aunt Caroline sent three years ago. Don't you see?"

"Why, yes!" said the happy creature, with a smile; "and they're all as new now as if they were in the store and not bought yet! Nancy, if it's a little gilded tea-set like that

Mrs. Blount brought home for her little granddaughter from France, won't you play tea-party with me once? You know I can't have any little girls to play with me while mamma is so sick."

"I guess I will play tea with you, and I'll bake pies and cakes just big enough to match the dishes," replied Nancy, laughing till the tears ran down her plump, crimson cheeks. "And I'll do more'n that: I'll make the folks at the table play tea out of them once, at any rate. You shall sit at the waiter and pour out tea for your grandma and for your papa, and *I'll* see that they both drink it!"

"Wouldn't that be funny!" cried the happy child, clapping her little hands. "But would it be polite to *make* an old lady play with a little girl?"

"Oh, la, yes, child; people must learn to be like children when they're where children is," said Nancy.

"Do you believe grandma would laugh?" asked Maggie.

"We'd *make* her laugh; it would do her good and make her happier, too," said Nancy.

"But oh, Nancy, suppose my present should be a silk dress or a new bonnet! Wouldn't that be dreadful? You know I don't care for fine things, and pa and ma and you think I look just as sweet, and sweeter, too, when I'm neat and clean than when I'm dressed up like a doll."

"Well, I'll tell you: if there isn't a set of china, after all the calculations we've been makin' to have tea-parties, I'll just go into Captain Blount's and look at Blossom's, and then I'll send for one by the store-keeper to Boston, as near like them as Boston can afford. I will, if it costs me a fortnight's wages; for you don't have money spent on you as some do, that ain't half so dear and good as you."

"Oh, Nancy, how kind you are!" exclaimed Maggie. "How I do wish you had never grown big, but stayed a little girl, just such as when you used to live with Grandma

Hale. Wouldn't you and I have nice times now?"

"Yes, dear; but then if I was a simple girl of twelve years, who would cook for you all, and wash your clothes, and lift poor, sick mamma softly in their strong arms, and get up in the night to give her medicine, not to disturb poor papa and make his head ache so that he couldn't study his sermons? I guess poor Nancy is good for more as she is, than she would be if she was only a foolish little playmate for you."

"I think so, too," said Maggie; and laying her curly head down on the broad shoulder of her humble friend, she added, in a subdued voice, "What should I do *now*, Nancy, without you?"

"Oh, God would provide for you, dear, if I was dead."

"But if you don't *die*, you'll always stay with me won't you? It would break my heart to have any lady take you away."

"I guess so, child; but what put that in your head?"

"Oh, that night that papa married big Mellissa Drake, I heard her husband tell him that he had so many children to be taken care of, and so much hard work to be done on his farm, that he thought the best thing he could do would be to marry a smart, tough woman to help him. I couldn't sleep, I was so afraid some man would want to marry *you*. You ain't half so big nor so old, and you are a *great deal handsomer* than she is! Now, Nancy, promise me that you won't get married if anybody should want you."

Nancy laughed heartily. "I can't make no rash promises, child," she said, "but I never had such a thought in my life; nor I don't never expect to have. But if a prince should come along in a pumpkin chariot with six mice turned into horses and take me off, like Cinderella in the story-book, you shall go too! No, dear: poor Nancy never expects to leave you till she goes to heaven. But just see who this is looking for you. Here's your dear father, with his big hat on, and his basket and hammer, calling, 'Maggie!' I guess he's going up to crack the stones in the mountains!"

"Maggie! Maggie."

"Yes, father dear, I'm coming," shouted the little girl, as with broad hat on her arm and her curls floating in the breeze, she ran to meet him at the gate.

They walked on some time in silence toward the rocky eminence behind the cottage.

"Why don't you talk, Maggie?" asked her father. "You generally have some questions to ask when we are alone together."

'I was thinking of one when you spoke, papa," said the child, "and my lips were half-open to ask it; but I was afraid it wouldn't be just right in mo."

"What is it, my love?"

"Were you ever naughty when you were young, so as to grieve poor grandma and make her cry?"

Mr. Bond smiled at the artless question.

"Yes, my dear, I am sorry to say that I very often did things which were wrong. I disobeyed my mother many times, and it makes me sad to think of it, and leads me to do all in my power to atone for it by kindness to her now. I hope you will help me in this work, and treat my mother very tenderly. She was a good mother to me, Maggie, and trained me up to fear God, so that I owe her a great debt of gratitude. Besides this, she is growing old, and therefore should be treated with great respect. As you read your Bible more and more, you will see how tenderly the great God speaks from heaven of the aged—the hoary-headed; and nothing displeases him more than to see the young and happy ridicule these or deal unkindly with them. The gray head is a crown of glory to those who walk in the ways of righteousness."

"What kind of naughty things did you do to grieve her, papa, when you were a boy?"

"Oh, sometimes I used to go fishing and

bathing in places she considered dangerous; and once, when she had forbidden me to mount strange horses, I hired one at a stable and rode off many miles with the naughty boy who tempted me to do it."

"Was grandma crying about it when you came back?"

"No, my love; I cannot remember ever having seen my mother shed a tear in my life. She was always a very strong woman—unlike your dear mother—and could endure a great deal more trouble without being made sick by it."

"Did you never see her cry? Then I guess nobody ever did when you were young. I've seen my mother shed tears when people died or had trouble, even if they were no relations to us."

"Well, dear, your mother and mine are very different; both would do a great deal to remove sorrow, although one might do it with tears and the other without."

"But, papa, did you never do any *very*

wicked thing for which grandma could't quite forgive you?"

"Oh, I hope not, my dear. God in his mercy has always kept me from open sin; and although there has been much that was unholy in my heart from childhood to the present time, yet I have been what the world would call a moral man and a good, affectionate son. Why did you ask that question?"

"Because it troubled me, dear father. I was *sure* that you were the best man in the world, and yet grandma seems all the time grieved with you."

"Oh, no! I don't think so, my daughter. She never says so to me."

"But she told poor Betsy Simpson that she had seen a great deal of trouble worse than grandpa's death, and that it all came through her children. She said you had forsaken her in her old age, and done *something* which would grieve the Pilgrim Fathers very much if they were alive to know it—something which none of their descendants ever did but you. I was so sad that I could hardly help crying, and kept trying to braid the fringe of my shawl and to think about something else to keep back the tears in Betsy's room. It has troubled me ever since, and yet I thought you might be displeased with me for asking what she meant."

Mr. Bond felt it difficult to explain the matter to his child, doing justice to himself and his principles, without making his mother appear narrow-minded and bigoted; but he could not help laughing at his imaginary sin against those who upon our shores

"Sought a faith's pure shrine."

"Maggie," said Mr. Bond, "you have heard little of the controversies among different Christians. But you know that all good people do not agree on every point. There is Mr. Bolton, the Congregationalist minister, whom I love as a brother, and who I believe to be a true and humble Christian; and our good neighbor, Mr. Talcot, of the Methodist church, pious and sincere; and here is your father, pastor of a Baptist church. Now, if I really believed these two good men preached the *whole* truth of God, and practiced his ordinances *just as Jesus commanded,* I would not stay here trying amid so many discouragements to build up a Baptist church. The other two meeting-houses would hold all who go to the three. I would go and preach the gospel where the people are not so well provided for. But as it is, I think it is my duty to remain and tell the people *just* what Jesus, my blessed Saviour, bade me tell them."

"Oh, papa! I'm so glad it *is* your duty to stay here," exclaimed little Maggie. "It doesn't seem to me that I could live anywhere else but just here by this old mountain, and among our own birds and flowers! Come, papa, we have walked a very long way: let us sit down here on our old fallen tree—I call this my sofa—and rest, while you tell me more about Jesus, and *just* what he wishes you to tell the people."

Mr. Bond took a seat, and laid his basket, which had as yet received neither a mineral nor a blossom, on the mossy ground beside him.

"Well, my dear, you see there are some important points on which Christians differ, or there would not be three churches here, all of whom love the Saviour and strive to honor him. Some good people are *ignorant* as to what Jesus teaches; some are *prejudiced;* while others are stupid or thoughtless, never examining any subject for themselves, but glad to be relieved of that trouble by believing whatever their parents or ministers teach them. Others again there are who mean well, but who think it makes little difference what we believe or practice, if we are only sincere and try to live about right. Jesus has left us certain commands, and bidden us to obey them *if we love him.* Some of these may seem small to us, but they are important in the eye of the Saviour, as tests of your love to him. He has left word for us to do *whatsoever he has commanded,* and it is as much sin in us to refuse to do what we call a *small thing* as what seems to our judgment of more importance. Do you understand that, Maggie?"

"Certainly I do, papa, and I wonder how any one who has a new heart and loves Jesus can refuse to do any thing he bids them. *I* never will, when I'm a Christian," said the artless child.

"Ah, Maggie, my dear, you will find that you have an evil heart even when God renews it; as I trust he will by his Holy Spirit. But about obeying him in what men call 'little things'—there were some thoughts I wished to impress on your mind. Suppose I should say to you some day, 'My daughter, bring a glass of water to my study;' but you should reply, 'No, father, I want to obey you, but a glass of water is such a *little thing* it is no matter whether I carry it up-stairs or not. I will not do *that,* but I will take up your gold watch here, that is worth something.' Would that be obedience to my commands?"

"No, papa; it would be very naughty. I would never say that; and if you told me to bring you a pin, I ought to take *just that* to you and nothing else."

"That's it, my daughter," said Mr. Bond. "I see that you understand what I am talking to you about."

"Oh, papa, it's so pleasant to sit here in the shade and listen to you! How I do wish mamma could come with us as she used to do last summer; don't you?" said Maggie.

"Indeed I do, my dear; but if she who is suffering so much in her lonely chamber is cheerful and patient, we must be so, although deprived of her company," answered her father. "Well, Maggie, we will suppose another case where obedience would be a proof of love. If your mother and I felt that we should both die soon and leave you an orphan, we should desire above all things never to be forgotten by our only, beloved child. To secure this remembrance of our affection, of our countenance and our form, so that neither the amusements of childhood nor yet the cares of after-life could ever obliterate them, we might say to you, 'Maggie, we are going away from you to our beautiful home above, where we hope to meet you when the Saviour calls you from earth. But until that time comes we want you to keep our memory fresh, even should you live to be a very old woman; and therefore we are going to leave with you a request which, whenever you comply with it, will bring your father and mother to mind.' Should you understand that?"

"Certainly, dear father; and whatever you wished me to do, I *would* with all my heart as long as I lived," replied the sweet child, with love beaming from her bright eyes.

"We might ask you to go once a year—perhaps on your birthday—and plant a little willow in our family cemetery, and then, sitting down beside our graves, to think of all our love, and of our happy home-days when God suffered us to dwell together a blessed family band, as he now does. Should you think that a very hard request?"

"No, indeed," replied Maggie. "I would do a thousand times more than that out of love for you, and so would any good child."

"Well, suppose you should do as we asked for several years, and your little trees of remembrance should strike deep roots and put forth green sprouts, and begin to cast cool shadows over our graves—"

"Oh, how I should love those willows! They would seem almost like friends who knew and loved you," interposed the eager young listener.

"Well," continued her father, "after a few years childhood would pass away, and maidenhood would come with all its pleasures. Perhaps as your birthday drew near and you were preparing to plant another willow twig, some friends might urge you to join them in an excursion to the sea-shore. You would tell them of the sacred duty which required your attention. 'Oh,' one would say, 'do that any other day.' What would you reply?"

"I would say," answered Maggie, "my dear, dead parents requested me to go to their graves, to think of them, and to plant a little willow every birthday as long as I live; and *I shall go that day.*"

"Well," continued Mr. Bond, "one of them might urge you thus: 'There are no willows near here, but plenty of young elms: an elm is as good as a willow and a great deal finer tree. If you rise early you can put out an elm, and then go with us afterward.' What would you say?"

"I would say, 'Those dear ones that I loved so much bade me plant a *willow*, and I will plant nothing but a *willow*, if I have to walk twenty miles to get one, and then bring it home myself!' I wouldn't have such friends, papa."

Mr. Bond smiled at Maggie's earnestness, as he said in his heart, "There is the old Brewster firmness and energy; God guide it aright!

But," he added aloud, "they may be on the whole worthy young people, and you might love their society. They would urge you to yield to them, saying, 'Your parents did not care more for a willow than for an elm; they only wanted you to plant *something* in the ground which would prevent your forgetting them.' You might follow the advice and—"

"No, I wouldn't, papa: I'd plant the *willow* twig and that *only*," said Maggie, bringing down her little foot resolutely on the mossy earth beneath her.

"But we'll *suppose* that you did—"

"But, papa, I don't even like you to suppose it, because I wouldn't!" insisted the child.

"Well, then, we'll let it be some other child of whom the request was made, and not Maggie Bond at all. She yields the first year, plants a young elm, gains an hour or two of time, and with few thoughts of the dead goes off with her friends. That very act has its effect on her own heart, and in a measure cooled the ardor of her love for the departed. She feels a little guilty, and does not love to think about them as much as before. When the next birthday comes she needs no tempter save her own heart, which says, 'It is a great deal of trouble to get a young willow, and an elm is no more what my parents bade me plant than a shrub is: I will put out a rose-bush.' The next year perhaps a crocus-bulb is more convenient, so she buries that between the graves; and now disobedience having gradually hardened her heart, she almost forgets the spot when the time comes round, and as she advances toward womanhood, the faces of those who watched so lovingly over her infancy fade like the pictures of a dream from her mind. After years of absence she comes back, a matron, to her native place, bringing her children with her, and takes them to the grave where their grandparents sleep. But instead of the close row of willows which they had hoped would one day fringe the sides of the cemetery, the children see only two or three willows, an elm, and a worm-eaten rose-bush. Do you think this mother would confess her forgetfulness and ingratitude to her children?"

"No, sir; she'd be ashamed of herself, and I should think she ought to be," replied Maggie.

"It is not like our proud nature to confess sin and then strive to atone for it. Should one of her sons say, 'Mother, this is a deserted, neglected spot: let us, from common respect to the dead, plant a few more willows around the wall and improve the place;' she would very likely be offended, and to take his remark as a reflection on her own filial love. Well, my love, you have a better friend than even your parents—Jesus, who has gone above. He has left his will written plainly in his word, and commanded us to obey him *in all things*. He bids us walk in his footsteps, and keep his ordinances *just as he has given them*. It is very dangerous to try to improve his work, for the sake of our own ease, or of taking away the reproach which the world fixes upon the simple rites of our holy faith. Maggie, whether we live or die, I wish you to remember this conversation about the willows, and it may aid you in some hour of trial. Make it a rule of your life, my darling, to ascertain *exactly* what the Saviour requires of you, and then do it, although it should cost you your life. They who suffer with Jesus, Maggie, shall also reign with him. Will you remember all this?"

"Yes, papa, I never forget any thing; Nancy says I never do. I will try to obey you and to do every thing Jesus bids me, too."

"But, Maggie, the sun is sinking, and we must hasten home, or dear mother will wonder where we are. Yet I wish to answer your question, which led to this conversation, 'What I have done to grieve my dear mother.' I will tell you all about it as we walk along.

"Jesus said to John the Baptist, *'Thus it becometh us to fulfill all righteousness,' and was baptized of him in the river of Jordan.* The baptism of believers is called *a burial,* which could not be done with a few drops of water. Philip went *down* into the water with the eunuch and came *up out of it* with him, showing that he could not have used a bowl for the purpose. John the Baptist baptized at Enon, 'because there was *much* water there;' if a few drops had sufficed, they could have done it anywhere. In Samaria they were baptized, 'both men and women, confessing their sins;' not a word about the babies, who were not conscious of sin. This then is our belief—that Jesus was baptized by having his body immersed in water, and that he commands us who love him to do the same. We know that this continued to be the general practice for thirteen hundred years after Christ. Sprinkling was introduced, by way of convenience, in what were termed cases of urgent necessity, such as sickness and approaching death. There is no account of baby-baptism for one hundred and sixty years after Christ; and then, and long after, it was generally opposed, as contrary to Scripture. It crept in, along with other errors and corruptions, from a superstitious notion of its being a saving ordinance; and as sprinkling was the easiest, that was adopted, except in the Greek church. The opinion that baptized children are somehow better off and safer than others, still prevails, even in New England, and it is a very dangerous error. There was our friend Mr. Johnson, you know, a member of Rev. Mr. Bolton's 'orthodox' church, who had his babe sprinkled an hour or two before it died. We believe that all who die in infancy are saved through the blood of Christ; and a few drops of water, or even immersion, could not make them safer. But you see, my child, that if the baptism of infants makes their salvation more certain, the millions of unbaptized children are left in a fearful state, if they die at that early age, which is a dreadful doctrine, and without warrant in God's word. Baptism is good and important in its place, as a profession of one's own faith in Christ, and as an act of obedience to his command; but great harm comes from any deviation from the Bible precepts respecting it. Christ enjoined immersion; but men have *altered* and *added*, until baptism is with many a very different thing from what was appointed. Instead of *immersion* we have *sprinkling* or *pouring*, and in addition to *believers*, *infant children* are brought forward as fit subjects of baptism. And thus children grow up to think themselves Christians, and, in some cases, members of tho church, just because they have been sprinkled by a minister. I know that my good mother does not accept all these errors that grow out of sprinkling and infant-sprinkling, but they are the natural fruit of those perversions of baptism. Something else will do in the place of what Jesus commanded. And now because *I* chose to search the Bible for myself, and to follow my Master in being buried with him by baptism, poor, dear

CHAPTER VII.

WHY, Endicott Cotton! my dear son!" exclaimed Madam Bond, as they entered the sitting-room of the parsonage, where supper awaited them; "I really thought you were lost; and that poor child looks more like a young Indian—between sun and wind and dust—than she does like a white child—a Brewster! Poor, neglected thing! how she is dragged about like a young mountain-ranger! Ah, she's beginning already to feel what it is to be motherless!" and the old lady looked at Maggie with all the compassion which could possibly be forced out of those iron gray eyes, even had the heart been full to overflowing of that grace.

Come here, my little Brownie," cried Mr. Bond, holding out his arms to the child. Maggie ran to him and sprang upon his knee.

Morning Gleam.

Page 117.

Her father untied the strings of her broad hat, which grandma had dignified with the name of "Margaret's umbrella," and holding back her tangled curls said, "Now come here and look at this face, mother. I suspect you think it a very plain little face, but I know a gentleman and lady who think it the dearest little face in the world; and that two or three additional coats of tan wouldn't have the power to spoil its beauty."

Maggie, in her artless innocence, put up her hands to assist in exposing her face for inspection, and turned round full before Madam Bond.

"Well, I declare," cried the old lady, "there's a strong resemblance, with her hair in that style, to Lady Hope Brewster, whose portrait is in our family. She was a strong woman, a heroine of the faith. It was said of her—so says the family tradition, which has, you know, come down with the picture—

'Beneath an angel's form
She bore a lion's heart.'

Why, the longer I look at this child the stronger the likeness grows! Endicott, you shall have that picture when I'm done with it, for I'm sorry to say Caroline does not set the value of a straw on it. Oh, Caroline hasn't a drop of the Brewster blood in her veins, nor a particle of noble pride in her ancestry! She has wounded my feelings many times on this subject, which you know is a tender one with me."

Maggie was still holding her hair up from its roots, hoping, probably, to gratify grandma, till it drew her eyebrows up and gave her a fierce, wild expression.

"There, love, you need not play Puritan maiden any longer," said her father, "but prepare for tea."

"Don't speak so irreverently before the child, my son," exclaimed madam, in an imploring tone. "I wish her to remain till I finish what I was telling you about my honored ancestor, that cultivated lady and noble-souled Christian. It is told of her that one night, when her husband and the men-servants were absent, she heard a loud groaning under her chamber window. Those were troublous times, and it stood the settlers in hand to know whom they admitted into their dwellings, especially when the men were off with the firearms. They lived on Roxbury Neck, and not a few houses had been invaded there by the hostile Indians. The domestics of Lady Hope Brewster clung to her, frail and young as she was, imploring her as she loved her life not to regard the tones of suffering, lest some vile creature might get in through her tenderness and murder the whole family; and—"

"Do tell the end quick, grandma!" exclaimed Maggie, with glowing eye and burning cheek. "I'm so afraid our ancestor took him in and got killed with a tomahawk."

"You shall hear, if you'll only have patience, child," continued grandma. "Her maid-servants ran hither and thither, hiding themselves in every conceivable place. But her courage never failed. She, remembering the Scripture injunction, 'If thine enemy thirst, give him drink,' took a lantern in her hand and descended to the street-door. She drew back the heavy bolt, which grated in its rusty socket, and aroused the attention of the sufferer. I tell you they did not use such dainty polished locks and bolts and keys as they do in our own day. Well, the Lady Hope set her lantern down upon the door-step, and wondering how she could ever, by her own strength, get the wounded creature into the house, went up to where he lay moaning piteously. He strove to raise himself upon his elbow, but failing from weakness he cried out, 'Friend, will thee give a dying man a shelter from the storm, till he can send for the wife of his bosom to close his eyes, and God will remember thee when thou comest into conflict with thy last and mightiest foes?'"

"Why," cried Maggie, "he talked just like our friend Obediah Collins. I do believe he was a Quaker! Of course she let him in, for the Friends are very harmless and kind. Everybody likes them."

"Of course? Indeed she did not let him in! Quakers of that day—whatever change may have come over them since—were pestilent fellows, disturbing the peace and breaking, for conscience's sake, as they termed it, the laws of the land.

"'Man,' she said, seizing her lantern and examining the cut of his coat, 'You are an enemy of God, a reviler of the righteous, a sower of seditions, and dare you ask a daughter of the Lord, against whom you are constantly rebelling, to harbor you beneath her roof? I verily thought you a red man of the forest, who, perchance, never knew God, and thus sinned unwittingly against his people;'" and grandma drew up her tall form in conscious pride that she had descended from this lion-hearted "Hope."

"I'm glad that is only a tradition, mother," said Mr. Bond, "and one, too, with feeble evidence to sustain it; for I should be ashamed of my ancestors could I believe that one of them was so lost to all feelings of mercy."

"Why, Endicott, you interrupt me so that I cannot finish my story. The tradition says the sick man proved to be a Quaker of the most seditious sort, who had disturbed the church, and given a great deal of trouble to the magistrates."

"Mother, I don't care if it had been Barrabas, the religion of Christ required her to feed and shelter him. What did she do with the passage of Scripture she had just quoted to her maid-servants when she thought the sick man an Indian—'If thine enemy hunger, feed him; if he thirst, give him drink?'"

"Endicott, that reads '*thine* enemy;' she could have forgiven him if that were all, and by kindness heaped coals of fire on his head; but these Quakers were the *Lord's* enemies. Don't you, can't you see the difference, my son?"

"Yes, mother, I do see that she looked on the red man with the eye of mercy, and on the dying Quaker with that of a stony-hearted bigot."

"These Quakers were enemies of *God*, Endicott."

"Well, then, she should have remembered that he had said, 'Vengeance is mine: I will repay.'"

"Did she let him die out on the side-walk in the rain alone?" asked Maggie, mournfully, with tears in her eyes.

"No, child; some government officers passing at the time helped him back to the prison whence he had just been discharged after another whipping, and he died there before break of day."

"Pa," said Maggie, drawing close to his chair, "I don't want to look like that woman: I hope you will never hold my curls up again as long as I live, and please ask grandma not to give us Lady Hope's portrait. I should think of the poor Quaker every time I looked at it."

"It is a very fine old painting, taken in

England, whither Lady Hope returned before her death," said madam, with a wounded tone.

"I should think it would bring a high price as a relic of those old times, if it could be proved genuine," said Mr. Bond. "But this Lady Hope is unknown in history, and great doubt hangs over such traditional characters."

"High price!" exclaimed grandma; "I would as soon sell my birthright for a mess of pottage as to part with that for money! I am grieved that neither of you set a proper value on it. Mr. Percy calls it a 'daub,' Caroline calls it 'Mother's Quaker-killer,' and you have no pride in any thing of the kind, Endicott."

"Well, dear mother," said Mr. Bond, "had that dying man been a Baptist, instead of a Quaker, he would have met with the same reception at the door of Lady Hope, if such a lady ever lived; now should such days ever return again, would you justify any one who treated your son thus, because, with the eye of Jesus, his Master, upon him, he can be nothing else but a Baptist?"

"Those days never will return," replied Madam Bond, evasively; "and here we are keeping Nancy's tea waiting by our long discussion. Margaret, as soon as you have washed and untangled your hair we will sit down, for I should think you and your father were about exhausted by that wild tramp of yours. Endicott, why won't you let me cut off that child's curls?"

"Because we love to look at them—her mother and I; and if she seems so homely to *you now,* she would appear far more so without them."

"I never *said* she was plain; but I'm sure she'll never be so handsome as her mother. Rebekah is to my taste a real beauty—or was when in health. Her daughter looks more like the old Hales." Mr. Bond smiled at the keen relish with which his mother always expressed her ire against the innocent couple to whose charge she laid the sin of his heresy, when the truth was that they never knew of the change in his sentiments until they had given him the jewel of their heart—the light of the parsonage.

"I shall not attempt to deny, mother," said Mr. Bond, as Maggie ran out to prepare for tea, "that my child looks like her grandfather Hale, and that therefore she is not a beauty; but she has a face which reveals intellect, and I feel sure she will make a good, strong, whole-souled woman. My ambition for her is that she may be of that class to which Paul refers, 'Those women who labored with me in the gospel.' I want her to be a toiler in my Master's vineyard. I doubt very much if my poor little girl will long have any duties to keep her at home. Soon, very soon, dear mother, there will be no household here to require an angel—none to need her affectionate ministrations. Far rather would I look forward and see her, when we are laid low, taking up the holy work we have left unfinished, than to see her an ornament of the gay world. Her mother and I have in prayer and faith given her to God, consecrated her to his service—a living sacrifice upon his altar; and the training you think so useless may be just what she will need when her work begins. Our first duty—after care for her soul—is to give her, as far as in our power to do it, a sound, vigorous constitution, and the cheerful spirit which usually accompanies that. She may be fitting herself by these long mountain-rambles and this out-door work for untiring labors among the jungles of India. I don't know what use God will make of her, but I do believe he will forbid her being either a drone in his hive or a butterfly outside."

"There, my son," cried Madam Bond, "don't talk so. Don't put such notions in her head, or she will devote herself to missions before she is converted, just from romance and love of adventure. She fears nothing, but rather courts hardship. If you and Rebekah *should* both go before us, it would be cruelty in the extreme to put any thing of the kind in her mind. She is the only child in the family, and we all love her and should look to her to soothe our declining years. I believe Mr. Percy and Caroline love her almost as if she were their own, although they have seen so little of her. I should say, if it were of any use, that *I* love her too; but you always seem to think I dislike the child, and it is very painful to me, Endicott. I consider her an unusually good little girl," added grandma, in a voice which betrayed no little emotion.

"Dear mother," replied her son, "I know you love Maggie and would make any sacrifice for her good, but I have thought sometimes that you did not make quite enough allowance for the folly of her early years—that you did not condescend enough to her low estate. But that she was dear to you for my sake as well as her own, I never doubted."

"I will appeal to Nancy," said Madam Bond—the faithful woman was passing through the room to relieve Maggie, who sat by her mother's bed—"whether I have not always spoken kindly to Margaret—whether I have not always been tender toward her."

"Nancy, as well as the rest of us, knows that you have, dear mother. Now send Maggie down and let us have tea: we are an hour past our time."

"But let Nancy reply to me," said madam, who seemed pleading innocence against an accusation of cruelty toward her granddaughter. "Did you ever see me treat Margaret any other way than with kindness?"

"Why, ma'am, I can't say," returned Nancy, "that ever I thought you one of them that was foolishly proud of children, so as to spoil them by indulgence. But you've been clever enough to *ours*. To be sure I have thought you a little *harsh* about them presents Mrs. Percy sent her. Five weeks has passed and she knows the trunks has been opened, and that they're somewhere where she can't get 'em. It's more'n one of Job's girls could 'a bore, and yet she hasn't mentioned 'em to me for a fortnight!"

Madam's cheek flushed. "Really, Nancy, you are right in that matter. I had entirely forgotten that I had a package for the child. I will get them after tea."

"Better get 'em '*afore*," said Nancy, who never quailed before dignities; "and then they won't be forgotten. What be they, if I may make so bold?"

Madam Bond seemed unusually softened and meek, and in no way did she resent the undue familiarity of the independent Nancy.

"*I* brought her a package of books, myself—"

"That's good, so far. She's a dreadful child for pretty books," interrupted Nancy, as if she had been appointed judge to pronounce upon the wisdom of the selection.

"And," continued madam, "I believe Mr. Percy sent her a blue-bird he brought from Paris, with machinery which, when wound up, makes it open its beak, raise its wings, and sing. It's a pretty thing, but I was really ashamed of Mr. Percy and Caroline: they acted like two children with it. It is much more suitable for Margaret. I think Caroline sent her a set of dishes, a couple of dolls, and some things to wear."

"She didn't!" exclaimed Nancy, laughing till the tears ran. "Well, that is queer enough! Maggie said—the dear child—that she hoped her present from Aunt Caroline would be a tea-set. Please, madam, to give the books to-night; but it's too late for the other things. She would get so stirred up that she wouldn't get to sleep till midnight!"

Just then the subject of Nancy's remark came bounding into the room as fresh as if she had not walked a mile, saying that mamma wanted them to take tea, and that if Nancy was busy she would lie alone for a little while. The nurse darted from the door like one guilty of great neglect, which she was desirous of atoning for; and the little family-group sat down to partake of their long-delayed evening meal. This being over and the things removed, Madam Bond, smarting beneath an imaginary accusation of not cherishing maternal affection for her only grandchild, rose and went toward her.

"Margaret, child," she said, "have you forgotten that I have some little treasures in my trunk for you?"

"No, grandma, I have not forgotten it," replied the child.

"Then why have you not asked for them?"

"Because I wanted to let you see that I could *wait.* My mother was always patient when she was a child, and never teazed, and everybody loved her. I want to be just like my mother."

"Well, Margaret, you're a good child. I'll give you what *I* brought you," and the old lady disappeared from the sitting-room on her mission to the dark closet, where she had imprisoned her trunks. She soon returned with a package, sealed in a most glowing and mysterious manner with red wax, and tied firmly with red tape. This on the buff wrapping-paper was calculated to make no small impression on the mind of a little girl of nine or ten years; and Maggie's bright eyes grew brighter as knot after knot was loosened, and seal after seal broken with most provoking coolness and deliberation. Nancy, an interested witness of the scene, stood in the door-way watching the process, when, the bonds being broken, the parcel fell afloat, revealing a wealth of good little books, in paper covers, which had been supported on either side by those bound in boards. Maggie almost reached out her hand to these last in covers gilt on red and blue; but another instant she remembered her old lesson on patience and drew back.

"Take them, child," said Madam Bond, "they are your own; and enough for a year's reading for a wise little head like yours." And grandma actually patted Maggie's head in an affectionate way, and said in a soft tone,

"A nice little girl you are, as children go now-a-days."

Maggie was completely overcome by such unwonted tenderness, and felt much as she did when she first caught sight of the inner heart of good Nurse Green; and beginning at the book nearest her, she passed on from title page to title page, her color varying as she read, and an expression of mingled disappointment and patient submission settling over her face as she laid down the last.

"Thank you, grandma," she said, in a trembling voice.

"Well, how do you like my selection, Margaret?"

"They are very good books indeed," answered the child with a quivering lip.

"Did you ever see any of them, to know whether they are good or not?"

"Yes, ma'am. We have 'Abbott's Young Christian,' and 'The Life of Henry Martyn,' in papa's library, and I have *tried* to read them; then mamma has 'Mary Lundie Duncan,' and 'Lady Huntington,' and *sveen* copies of 'Pilgrim's Progress.' The little books about good children who *all died*, you sent me by Aunt Caroline two years ago. I read the first few pages of them all; but the words were pretty long and the thoughts pretty hard, and I laid them away till I grow up; but maybe I can understand them *now*. Thank you, grandma," said Maggie.

"Be they Track S'ciety books, if I may make so bold?" asked Nancy.

"Yes, Nancy; and *you* can read them too. They are not beneath the full-grown Christian —even the smallest of them," replied Madam Bond.

'Indeed they are not, ma'am; but a good many of them are *above* the little child. It would take an experimental Christian to understand some of the smallest of them. Maggie said, when her mother read some of them to her two years ago, that 'she wondered if all good children *had to die* so young!' She said she wanted to stay in this world and comfort her father and mother before she went to heaven to be happy herself."

Now Madam Bond had strict views of reading, and thought it very inconsistent in Christian parents to allow their children any books save such as were strictly religious. She thought it exceedingly wrong to illustrate any doctrine to their minds unless by *facts;* forgetting probably, good woman as she was, that Jesus began his teachings in a way to catch the ear and the attention of his hearers, by parables or narratives rather than by elaborate essays on the doctrines and practices of Christianity. Who imagines that when our blessed Master said, "Behold a sower went forth to sow," he had any particular man in his mind, of whom and the results of his labors he was giving a precise account?

It is not well to be wise above what is written, and we believe the best way to present the truths of the gospel to the minds of the young is that in which they can understand them, else the labor both to teacher and scholar is lost.

"No, Nancy," said Madam Bond, "I don't believe in presenting the gospel, with all its blessed teachings, like a bitter pill, and sugaring it over with a tale, to cheat the child into swallowing it. I think it should be presented as strong meat, and they made to believe it their duty to take it."

"Well, ma'am," said Nancy, "if you offer beef to a new-born baby it will do one of two things—it will either turn away from it and starve, or else it will take it and choke to death. So it is in teaching folks religion. I can speak from experience; for they say that old fools and wise children want about the same management. Oh, what beautiful ways my dear old Mistress Hale had of making us understand these things! True, we hadn't such lots of library-books as we have now, but she used to *make up* such sweet stories, besides tellin' us things that she knowed when she was young. I believe in makin' religion just as lovable as possible to the ignorant folks and to little children. Jesus did so when he was on earth. If them Jews hadn't had in 'em such evil hearts of unbelief, they wouldn't have stood out agin such preachin' and pleadin'; but would have taken him, poor as he was, right into their hearts and homes: But," she added, smiling, "I guess my talk won't make learned folks much wiser, so I may as well go about my work." And she vanished, singing

"Oh, how happy are they
Who their Saviour obey!"

"Well, Margaret," asked the grandmother, "is there any more I can do for you to-night, child?" This was probably to see if Maggie had strength to avoid asking for her gifts from Aunt Caroline.

"No, thank you, grandmother," replied the child.

"Did you not know that I had a little package for you beside the books?"

'Yes, ma'am."

"Then why haven't you asked for them to-night?"

"Because I wished you to see *that I knew how to wait,*" said Maggie, with a firm expression; "and besides that, grandmother, Nancy says it will do myself good, teaching me a lesson of patience, such as I would never have had a chance to learn if you had not come and hid my pretty presents away in the dark closets among the quilts and blankets."

An expression of pain passed over Mr. Bond's face as he laid down his newspaper and remarked, "Maggie has been the child of so much love that no one has deprived her of pleasure for the bare sake of teaching her submission. Our own joy has depended so much on seeing her happy that we have always gratified her when in our power. I am glad to see that it has not made her selfish or impertinent when brought under restraint."

"I'm sure, Endicott, she has never been

restrained nor her curiosity tantalized by me. At first I was too weary to unpack my trunks, and then I waited to be *asked* for the package, as Nancy told me Caroline had written about it; and as I had taken all I need from that trunk it entirely slipped my mind. I'm sure I do not take pleasure in disappointing the child."

'Certainly not, mother; no one could say so," replied her son.

"I will atone for my neglect by bringing them now, if you think best," said madam, half rising from her seat.

"No, mother. Nancy said, I think, it might disturb her rest. Maggie, my love, Aunt Caroline has sent you some fine things —one of them very rare—such as you never saw before; but father thinks you had better wait until after breakfast to-morrow to see them. Are you willing to do so?"

"Yes, father," replied the child. "The nights are not very long in summer, you know. I'll try to wait one more."

"She's certainly a good child," murmured grandma, as if for her own benefit only—"that no one can deny. Her submission speaks well for her training."

These words, low as was the tone in which they were uttered, did not escape the ear of Maggie, and she went to bed that night happier than she had done for a long time. She felt that in some unaccountable way she had gained the favor of her grandmother, and her little heart, ever yearning for love and approbation, felt a calmness and joy for which she could not account.

When Mr. Bond stepped into Maggie's room—as was his custom before retiring to rest—to see that she were sleeping sweetly, to his amazement he found her eyes as bright as if it were noonday.

"Why, my daughter! are you not sleeping after our long and wearisome walk? What makes you so wakeful, my love?" he asked.

"Oh, papa," replied the child, putting one

little arm around his neck, as he bent tenderly over her, "I'm so happy that I cannot sleep. I have to lie awake to think how glad I am."

"And what is it that makes you so happy, Maggie? Not your present of books, for I saw that you were a little disappointed in not getting new ones which you had not seen before."

"Oh, no, papa! I don't care so *very much* for the presents, although I shall be happy when I get auntie's; but what makes me so glad is that grandma, dear grandma, has *forgiven us.*"

"Forgiven whom, my love?"

"You and me, father."

"But, my dear Maggie, she was not offended with us; she had nothing to forgive."

"Hadn't she, father?" asked the child. "But I'm sure she loves us both more to-night than she ever did before. Didn't you see her lay her hand on my head so kindly—just like Grandma and Grandpapa Hale?

Didn't you hear her say I was a good child, and that you and mamma had trained me well? I shall never come in at the kitchen-door again for fear of meeting her in the front entry. Oh, I did want to lay my head on her shoulder and put both arms around her neck when I kissed her 'good-night,' but I was afraid it wouldn't please her. Still I feel so glad to-night that I cannot sleep."

Oh, how little it sometimes takes to make a young child happy! Is it not cruel, when a gentle word, a soft tone, an approving smile, can do it, that those should be wanting? Remember, ye who have, under God, the keeping of these young immortals' happiness, that the days of darkness are coming, and that they may be many. Make them glad while ye may.

"Ah, my dear little daughter," said Mr. Bond, "I fear you never lay wakeful upon your bed for gladness that *Jesus* had forgiven your sins—that he had spoken in gentle tones, saying, 'I have loved thee with an everlasting love'—that his hand lay in blessing upon your head, and his soft wing overshadowed your pillow. Did you, Maggie?"

"No, papa; because I never felt *really* that Jesus was displeased with me. I know I am not *all* his child—that I haven't a new heart; but I'm not *so very wicked,* papa. I never took God's name in vain, like poor Mose Sawyer; I never stole strawberries nor flowers nor melons, like poor Biddy O'Neil, who has no one to teach her right; I'm never saucy to people, like Jakey Smith; nor do I ever play on Sunday, as the children we pass on the railroad do."

"My child," said Mr. Bond, "your conscience does not accuse you of any great sin toward your *grandmother*—you have always tried to treat her respectfully and with attention. Neither has she ever laid you under any particular obligations. You have never needed to go to her for bread or garments or medicine, and yet you are overpowered with gratitude because she has spoken tenderly, and shown that she has no ill-feelings toward you. Maggie, there must be something wrong, very wrong, in your heart, which seems so good to yourself. What has not *Jesus* done to merit your love and gratitude? Who gave you birth in a Bible-land and a Christian family? Who has kept you alive, by giving you his air to breathe, his bread to eat, his water to quench your thirst? Who, above all other blessings, has given you the offer of life in heaven, and shed his own blood that you might live forever? And yet you, knowing that he has not forgiven your sins, and that you have never asked him in sincerity to do it, can lie down and sleep sweetly night after night, not having any pledge that you shall ever awake again on earth! God bless you, my precious child, and make you truly his own. God grant you many a night, in the years to come, in which you shall be 'so glad that you cannot sleep,' because he has spoken tenderly to you and forgiven your sins." And, with an embrace which combined a father's love and a mother's gentleness, Mr. Bond withdrew and left the little one to her own thoughts.

Morning Gleam.

PAGE 147.

CHAPTER VIII.

AFTER breakfast next morning the gifts of Uncle Percy and Aunt Caroline were duly exhibited and admired, and the blue-bird honored by making a short call on mamma, who was highly gratified by its wonderful feats.

The cups and saucers were of the most approved style and pattern, holding almost half as much tea as mamma's; and Nancy forewarned grandma and Mr. Bond that the day was not far distant when Maggie was to entertain them with a miniature tea-party, when she should be lady at the head of the table and they her company. All smiled approval of the plan, and Maggie asked, "And wouldn't it be pleasant for Nancy to carry dear mamma's supper up first, and let her eat from these dishes—it would *seem* as if she were playing with us too—wouldn't it? But do look down the avenue! There comes some one just like Bunyan's Pilgrim, with his burden on his back, and a great stick —*staff,* I mean—to lean upon; and he's looking up to Morning-Gleam Cottage as happily as if he had got almost to the Celestial City!"

"Certainly, Endicott," exclaimed Madam Bond, in a low tone, "that child grows wiser and wiser! Most children, if they had drawn a comparison at all, would have said that bag tied at the neck made them think of 'The malt that lay in the house that Jack built.' I *hope* she may *live;* but I don't know," added the old lady, with a mournful shake of the head: "such children seldom do."

"And oh, look, Nancy," continued Maggie, "I really believe he's got a roll in his hand. I almost think it is Christian. No, he looks too happy and too young for him. He couldn't smile so while he had the burden to carry. How rosy his cheeks are, and how light and curly his hair is! Who can he be, papa?"

"You will soon know, my love, for he is almost here. I rather think he is one of Auntie Bell's swift-footed messengers; he seems laden down as heavily as they usually are when they come to the parsonage."

"What *would* you do without that Mrs. Bell, my son?" inquired Madam Bond.

"I need not be anxious about that, mother, as every church has its 'Auntie Bell,' under one name or another. I believe God appoints to each these *ministering sisters* as much as he does the angels to the churches. Go where you will, to large or small branches of the true Vine, whether in city or wilderness, and ask the servant of Christ or his toil-worn companion, who it is that foresees their wants, bears their burdens, supplies their needs, sits by their sick-bed, and bears up their fainting spirits on the broad, pure wings of her beautiful faith? Each one will tell you, 'Oh, we have a sister in our church.' Yes, there is just such a sister in every church! When God calls one home, he raises up another. A holy ministration truly is theirs—'those women who labored with me in the gospel.' If I have built up this young church, if souls have been brought to God through my labors, *she* must wear the crown. But for her entreaties and encouragements I should long ago have entered another field. Oh, mother, you will not leave Morning-Gleam till you learn the worth of that woman."

A low tap at the side-door and Nancy admitted the pilgrim, who, with a modest bow and many blushes, approached Mr. Bond and laid his offering at his feet with these words: 'Your Reverence, Mrs. Bell send to you one bag crackers—in it ten pound white sugar. She tell me give you this little letter, and she tell you send by me how is de sweet lady sick up-stairs. And sair, my name Pierre Le Bonne, French boy from Ca-na-da."

"Take a seat, Pierre, my friend, until I read Mrs. Bell's note," said Mr. Bond; and, with a manner not a little restrained, the humble youth did as he was requested. Nancy, by virtue of her office, took possession of the crackers and vanished from the room; while grandma took a book, and Maggie busied herself about her canaries' cages.

"Pierre, my good boy," said the minister, rising and giving him his hand with a degree of cordiality unusual in a gentleman toward a poorly clad peasant; "I'm truly glad to see you. Let me take your hat, and then I will hear all the good things which Mrs. Bell says you have to tell me."

"I very 'shamed to trouble such a fine gentleman with my poor heart," said the youth, "but my kind friend—like mother to me—she tell, 'Reverence love trouble for Christ's sake, and his heart so glad when one poor French boy pray no more to *Virgin*, but go to *her Son*, and say to him, My Lord an' my God!'"

"Mother," said Mr. Bond, "if you will lay aside your 'Morning Exercises' for a little while, I think you will be edified by the conversation of this young stranger, thrown in a providential manner under the influence of our good Mrs. Bell."

Madam Bond graciously closed her book, laid her gold-bowed spectacles in the place where she had been reading, and took from her pocket a bit of work she was doing for her humble friend Betsy Simpson, and composed herself to listen.

"Now, Pierre, Mrs. Bell says you will give me your history, and then tell me on what points you need instruction and light. How long since you left Canada?"

"It is two year long since I leave my father's little cabin on the high bank of the St. Lawrence. Then I am sixteen year old that day; and my father have little work for his many boy to do, and they eat great deal of bread. Twelve children, boy and girl, in my one family; only one older as me, and he have lame place in the high top of his leg—he what you call crip-pel boy. So I say to my mother, 'I go off and get money far away on the sea, and Carlos'—he then fourteen year and good boy—'he chop logs with father, and cook the dinner, and hold the baby, and wash little faces, and sew up holes in the stockings, and every thing.'"

"Did you do all those things when you were at home, my good boy?" asked the minister.

"Oh, a great many more things as that I do for my good mother; and she cry her face very red when I go 'way from her," replied the artless Pierre.

"And where did you go at first?" asked Mr. Bond.

"First I go to Calais, and then in a lumber-vessel I go into the sea to B——. I get twelve dollar every month to cook for the men, till six months gono 'way; then I buy fifteen dollar of clothes, and all rest of money Captain Lowe put on paper when we get back here and send in letter to a good man four mile from my father's house. That man write letter that they bless their dear boy, and buy flour and meal and pork and flannel with my money. But no more that winter could I find vessel; so I will not go home to eat up their bread, and I ask everybody, 'Want a boy to work?' An old woman in the market in city say to me, 'Yes, my missus want a boy to make fire, scour floor, sift cinder, and shovel snow. If you steal not and get not drunk, she will give you four dollar all month of winter, and as much as you will eat.' That old woman was cook, and her missus keep grand boarding-house full of fine lady and gentleman."

"And did you go there, Pierre?" asked Mr. Bond.

"Yes, Reverence, she say to me, 'Come to-night or to-morrow;' but she have too heavy basket to carry; so I say, 'No, but I will go with you *now* and take home your load. I be one week and do no work; I will be glad to lift the meat and other thing for you.' So she laugh and say, 'Well, come home with me. I will take you into the kitchen with myself.' So when we go in she laugh to her missus and say, 'I found just the boy I want—not 'fraid of work;' and missus say, 'Glad, Sarah, for you work too hard.' To me she say, 'Be good boy, and Sarah will be friend to you.' Then she go up-stairs and bring me down good coat and pants and boots, and Sarah show me little room for myself, and I very happy, and tears come in my eyes when I thank cook and tell her how hard I will work for her."

"And you found this poor cook a good friend, did you?" asked Mr. Bond.

"Oh, sair, very good. When I thank her for bring poor strange French boy to a warm home from the street, she say, 'Thank not me, Peter'—she always call me *Peter*—'I go not out that day to find you. But God, the great Father, look down from heaven and see you with no home, and he sent you to me in the market; thank *him*.' 'Oh,' I say to her, 'I very, very good. I pray to our Blessed Lady two time every day and count my bead;' and then I show her my beads and this, which my mother gave me to keep the witches off and to save me from sinking when I on the sea, if my ship be loss." Here Pierre drew from his pocket a long rosary, composed of rose-wood beads linked together with plated rings, from the middle of which was suspended a plated cross and an image of our Saviour in his agony. This he passed respectfully to Madam Bond, and then offered the charm—a red morocco heart, *said* to enclose a piece of "the Virgin's bowels of mercy"—to the minister. "The first my mother bring with her from Avignon, in France, and the other she walk nine mile and pay ten shilling for, to Father Vogle, that I shall be safe on the sea."

"And had you not *common-sense* enough, young man," asked Madam Bond, who was apparently interested in his story, "to know that these things couldn't keep you from harm?"

"No, lady," replied the innocent Pierre, "I

had *no common-sense at all* till I meet with cook Sarah in market."

"She couldn't teach you *that*," replied madam

"Oh, yes, lady; I just like little dog—what I be teach I learn, and what I be not teach I know not."

"Well, Pierre," asked Mr. Bond, "how did poor Sarah teach you the way of life?"

"Oh, sair, she so full of pity for every thing! She see my soul blind, and she say to me, 'Poor boy, pray God to make you his child.' When little beggar come in, she sit her up in chair by fire and feed her, and warm her, and give her mittens. She knit at night when fine lady go to the dance, and she sit up to let her in, 'cause missus gone to bed sick with tired. Chamber-girl say *she* would not give beggar any thing, 'cause beggar's father drink the rum; but poor cook say, 'my father drink the rum too, and nobody warm me, nobody pity me; so I will care for poor little beggar-child.' Some day she be very tired when she work late. Then she take little black book off' shelf and read to *rest* self. Then the tired look all go way, and she look happy, and put up book and sing—oh, so sweet! One day I say to her, 'That book make you feel good: what tells it to you?' She say, 'All 'bout my blessed Jesus that come to this world to save the sinner. He say to poor me, *Come unto me and I will give you rest.* Oh, what rest that be! Oh, poor little Frenchie,' she say—all the people call me Frenchie—'Sarah wish you would throw 'way you foolish beads and come to her Jesus.' But, sair, I cannot read her book, and my heart ache when I look at it all time. I think Jesus, that rest good Sarah and make her full of pity and good, is in that book; but I can never find him. My bead and crucifix look poor and give me no comfort; when I go bed I sleep not, because Sarah tell me my soul not safe—that my charm cannot carry me to Jesus nor keep death far off. One day I sit all alone in kitchen, and I take down little black book and turn over leaf after leaf and say in myself, 'Oh, wish I could tell which of all these many words is the name *Jesus!*' Tears come in my eye and I say, 'loud out, 'Oh, Jesus, poor French boy try to find you, but he find not!' Sarah come in, and big tears in her eyes; and she say that every one that look for Jesus *shall* find him. She lay her hand on my head and say, 'God of the stranger, pity my poor dark-hearted boy. Take 'way all his bad and make him God's boy!' Then she take down the book and she show me 'Jesus;' she say, 'J-E-S-U-S; that make the blessed name.' So I turn over and over, and oh, I find many, many times 'Jesus,' and I want to cry out loud, 'My Jesus!' But my heart very sore, and I 'fraid, for Sarah tell he love not those who pray to bead and wear charms and love money or any thing more than him. So I know he love me not, and my heart cry out 'loud, 'What shall I do?' And she tell me go to my little room and say all time, 'Take me, Jesus—drive bead out of my heart;' and I throw 'way foolish things, and pray only to God, who make me and who send his dear Son to die for me.'"

Madam Bond had laid down her needlework and sat eying the humble stranger with real tenderness. When he paused for a moment, she asked, "And how did that good woman lead you on?"

"Yes, she lead me on, lady," replied the poor youth. "She teach me some words in that book: 'Who come unto me, I will not cast out;' then I say, 'Jesus, *I* come.' She tell me, 'Who knocks, the door shall be opened for him;' and I say, '*I* will knock at God's door and never go 'way till I die.' She tell me, 'Who believe shall be saved,' and I say, 'Oh, Jesus, poor French boy believe every word you say in the book, and believe none but yourself can save his soul, and believe, too, that you will do it!' Such thing she tell me, and then she sing to me,

'Jesus! I love his charming name,
His name is all my trust;
Nor will he put my soul to shame,
Nor let my hope be lost.'

And I sing out loud, too, although sing not very good; and missus come in kitchen and smile and say, 'Ah, Sarah, you and Frenchie turn Methodis?'

"Well, Sunday come, and all forenoon we have work; but after dinner fine gentleman try his horse, or smoke on portico, or lie on sofa; and fine lady all go to bed. So we do work quick and go to big church on hill. I sit in Sarah's pew in gallery and listen *so hard;* for my English very poor that time. Dr. Raymond, Sarah's minister, talk very nice and loud, but say very big word; poor me un'stand him not, only when he say, *Jesus, Jesus, Christ, Lord, God.* He say these, oh, many, many time, and *heaven,* and that worth more as money to me! I can sit all night just only to hear him say *Jesus,* and it seem to me before he get through it am all

Jesus. Then when he preach no more, he come down and put hand in silver bowl and baptize the face of one gentleman, two nice lady, and four baby—just like my old priest in Canada.

"When I go home, Sarah tell me how much do I un'stand. I tell her, 'Jesus, Jesus, and that enough now; I only want to hear that and no more. My poor heart so small it can hold no more as that till more days come.' When Sarah take the book and light the lamp, I tell her, 'Your priest have no cross, no bead, no host, like my old priest; but he baptize like my old priest. *You read me* Jesus baptized, and the *man* and the *woman* baptized; but you read not to me where the *baby too* be baptized, and you not read me my priest's way to baptize. Your book say, Go into the river and be baptized.' Then she tell, 'Oh, I poor ignorant old woman and know no more at all. I can't find the place where it tells to sprinkle water in baby-face —*never could;* but it *must be there,* for my minister knows every thing, and he baptize the baby! Every day you learn little more, Pierre, and by-and-by we come to that place, and we'll ask Dr. Raymond too—he tell us.'"

"Then she was teaching you to read, was she?" asked Madam Bond, who began to nestle about a little, and put on her glasses again, preparatory to reading out her chapter in *Jay's Morning Exercises.*

"O, yes, lady, every day she teach me; and one day missus say, 'The black book too hard;' and when she go out she bring in the spell-book and slate and pencil for me. Oh, I feel so good then the tears come; and every day then I learn much fast. Missus write little mark and then little word, and then I write and write till ten, 'lefen 'clock, all nights, and when snow all gone I write small letters to my mother in Canada. Oh, I must go soon to them and tell them 'bout my new religion I found. Then they all believe and love my Jesus too!"

"And how came you to leave your good place, Pierre?" asked the minister.

"Oh, sair, they want not boy when no snow to be shoveled, no coal put in cellar and carry up-stairs; so they sew my clothes all mend and clean, and missus give me carpet-bag and every thing, and I come in country to look for work on a farm. I call at house, house, many house, and all tell me, 'No, got all man I want.' Dark night come and I stop at Mr. Bell's, and he say, 'No,' too; but lady come out, and she say me, 'Stranger?' and I tell her, 'Yes.' 'Got any place to sleep?' I tell her 'No;' so she say, 'I got bed for stranger, and bread for stranger;' so I stay there. Next day she talk to me, and then Mr. Bell say he will *make* work for me; so I thin out the trees in grove and clear under-brush, and I very happy indeed here." And he laid his hand on his heart. "They do sing, and they do pray, and they do love my Jesus there in that house."

"And you and Mrs. Bell found that

although you had never met before, you belonged to one family; that you were both the children of God, and that Jesus is your brother? I suppose you both talked together of heavenly things," said Mr. Bond.

"Yes, sair," replied the good youth. "I tell that lady all my heart; then I ask her all her heart, and say, 'What you call your church?' She say, 'Baptist;' and I know not what is Baptist. Then she tell, 'Jesus was baptized of John in Jordan, and people was baptized where was *much water;* and Philip go down into water and come up out of water when he baptize eunuch; and they were baptize, *men and women, confessing* their sins;' she say, 'Like as her Master tell her—like as he set example, so she do.' She say, 'Cook Sarah's book all true,' and *that* havo no word 'bout baptize in the bowl—no word 'bout baptize poor little baby cannot confess sin, cannot know any thing; that Jesus' brethren and sister *must* 'bey his command, and will if they love him. Poor French boy wonder much 'bout Baptists; for I know not there be such a named people in the world, yet, when I read New Testament, I say in my heart, 'Why do all minister put finger in bowl and call drops of water baptize?'"

"'The wayfaring man, though a fool, need not err,' if he seek to know the way," said the minister, "so plainly and simply has God revealed his will to us."

"I guess," said Madam Bond, tartly, "that somebody put that in his head! Are there no Baptists in Canada, young man?" she asked.

"I never hear of him there," replied the untutored youth; "I hear only of Catholic and Protestant."

"Well, my friend, you have a great deal to learn yet more important than that. The wisest scholars cannot agree on that knotty question; so you, without a knowledge of Greek, had better not try. Let mysteries alone, and don't be wise above what is written!"

"Thank you, ma'am—lady," returned Pierre, to whom the remarks were quite unintelligible, they having been uttered in a low voice, with the eyes, those great interpreters, bent on her work.

"You're right in the judgment you formed, my friend," said Mr. Bond, "and glad should you be that you in your ignorance have been taught of God. You have received your Father's command, while many, because of its very simplicity, turn away from it and seek to mystify it, so that it may be hidden under the vail of a dead language from the common people, who, in all ages, are the first to receive and obey gladly the message Jesus sends. Immersion in water—on profession of our faith in and love for Jesus—is the only baptism, and if you have really found Christ, as Mrs. Bell believes you have, it is your duty to arise and be baptized."

"So I will, sair; and *any thing else* my Jesus tells me, that I will do."

"Your champion will surely exert a great

influence through his theological learning!" said madam in a sarcastic tone, without looking up.

"I would rather have his unbiased opinion, founded on God's word, than that of many a learned professor who has a system to maintain. Learning and theological acumen are often used for a refuge in which to hide when met face to face by an unwelcome truth," said Mr. Bond.

"Ugh!" replied the old lady. "However, my son, I think the youth has been converted."

"And so do I, mother; and I am ready to lead him into the emblematic grave as soon as my church receives him," replied her son.

"It seems rather a want of Christian modesty, however, for him to come forward in his ignorance and set up his opinion over that of the greatest scholars of the age," said Madam Bond.

"He does not set up *his opinion:* it is the plain command of Jesus. And as to the greatest scholars of the age being on the other side, it is not admitted yet; and if it were, instead of defying them, I doubt very much if the poor fellow knows the name or the existence of one of them. Sometimes, you know, dear mother, God reveals things to babes which are hidden from the wise and prudent; and we must bow our pride and be willing to receive his truth in the same simplicity, or we cannot dwell in the light."

This conversation being held in a low tone, and not addressed to him, had about the same effect on the stranger as if he had been a deaf man; so he sat smiling on Mr. Bond, with whose condescension he seemed greatly delighted. He now rose to go, and Mr. Bond said, "I will see you again, my friend, at Mr. Bell's, and talk with you on this great subject;" and wishing them all "glad-morning," Pierre hastened off to his work in the grove.

"That is no stereotype experience," remarked Mr. Bond to his mother, "but a genuine work of grace described in nature's own words."

"It is certainly an interesting case, and I truly rejoice that the poor fellow has met with such a blessing; but really," continued the old lady, "I do wish some of your new converts were people of a higher class. I know, as well as you can tell me, that his soul and that of Betsy Simpson are as precious as those of the wisest of earth; but it does seem strange that you, with all your ability and learning and talent, should be drudging here to build up a church, when you might be settled among people of mind, and any ignoramus could interest these!"

"There you are greatly mistaken, my dear mother. Although the great majority of my people are plain in their dress and in their style of living, I will not admit that they are a whit behind any congregation in the region for intelligence or piety. And as to *any sort* of a minister answering for a young and struggling church—that is a great mistake too. Such need all the wisdom and influence that the wisest and best man can bring with him. I wish my people had a superior man for a pastor; or rather I would say, I wish their present one was superior to what he is; for it is my wish to spend and be spent for them. They are *my people*, bound to me by a thousand ties of love and gratitude, and I hope to live and die among them."

"Ugh! So I told Mr. Percy when he spoke of your going to the Walnut Street Church there. I told him you were so obstinate that were they to offer you four times what you had here, you would not go; for that you had prophesied a great, prosperous church of your *sect* here, and you would stay to fulfill the prophecy."

Mr. Bond smiled; but there was more of pain than pleasure in the smile. "You were quite right, dear mother, in saying that *money* could not woo me from the people of my first love; but I hope a better motive than to obstinately carry a point or build up a sect induces me to press on through all the difficulties which attend the establishment of a church, holding, as this does, unpopular sentiments, in a community where the main influence is in another direction. I firmly believe God has sent me here to preach *his truth,* and to administer his ordinances in the way of his own appointment."

"It must be a very comfortable feeling the Baptists all enjoy—that *they alone* have the truth," said Madam Bond. "I see how it is—'we are the people, and wisdom will die with us.'"

"It is a consolation, certainly, to feel that one has made great sacrifices for conscience-sake; but, so far from believing that wisdom will die with *me,* I think a good deal will be left in the world *if my mother survives me,*" said Mr. Bond, pleasantly. "Will you bear with your son, who loves you, while he asks you a question he has never asked?"

"Certainly, Endicott, I love to argue," replied Madam Bond.

"*I don't love to argue,* and am not going to begin it. I only want to ask if you ever said to your prejudices, 'Stay ye here till I go to the closet and the Bible and examine this subject under the eye of the Master, to whom I have sworn fealty in all things, great and small?' Have you ever done so, my dear mother?"

"No, nor do I ever mean to!" exclaimed Madam Bond, warmly. "Do you think, Endicott, that I am going to insult the memory of my father and grandfather and all my honored ancestors by *admitting* even that they were mistaken, and begin at this later day to pry into things they left settled? No, indeed!"

"Take care, dear mother," said Mr. Bond, smiling, "lest you get your foot planted on the Pope's ground and set up the infallibility of a church."

"Ugh! it is this prying curiosity to get hold of hidden mysteries which God has not chosen to reveal, which makes the Baptists so—so—"

"So *what,* mother, dear?" asked the gentleman, smiling.

"So *obstinate,* my son! There is a sort of consciousness of right and of superiority of judgment in the very face of every Baptist I ever met; this, with an expression of meek endurance, such as the old martyrs might have worn on their way to the stake, writes BAPTIST on their very brows. I can tell one when I meet him in the street! And when one wishes to argue a point with them, they say so cooly, 'Go to the New Testament—go to the New Testament,' as if it was made for *them.*"

"But why should not all Christians carry about this same stamp of the genuineness of their belief on their faces, if they are as sure of their ground as the Baptists are of theirs? They have the same right to do so. The truth is, dearest mother, you are not agreed among yourselves, now, as to the baptism of infants. One of your lights tells you it came in room of circumcision, thus, if consistent, cutting off all females from this privilege; another tells you it was an ordinance instituted when Jesus took little children in his arms and blessed them; and—"

"There, now; do stop, my son. *I hate arguments,* and will not go any farther. I shall hold on to my views, and you may, if you will be so obstinate, remain away from the church in which you were born—"

"I wasn't born *in a church,* mother: I was born in sin," said her son.

"And you may trample under foot the covenant I entered into for you at the baptismal font: I shall be clear. I wish now, finally, to wash my hands of all participation in your course. After this, if you go on in the road of changes, till you land in some great heresy, I shall feel clear of guilt."

"So you may, mother; you have done all you could to keep me in the old paths; but I hear a voice I cannot refuse, calling, '*This* is the way: walk ye in it.' How thankful I am that we shall dwell forever together where we shall see eye to eye, and where, all the mistakes and errors of life having been forgiven, we shall all be like our pattern," said Mr. Bond.

"Oh, then," asked the old lady, as if in surprise, but really in irony, "you Baptists intend to let other denominations into heaven, do you?"

"I hope," said Mr. Bond, "*we* shall be among those who are washed and sanctified and made meet for the inheritance of the saints in light. I sit in judgment on none, but must myself walk in the light God has shed around *me*. There is but one thing in all this world I cannot sacrifice to please my mother: that is, conscience. So, as we cannot agree in all our views, we will talk no more about our differences, but love and enjoy each other while we may."

"I'm sure I love you, Endicott; one would think, to hear you talk, that your mother was without natural affection!" said Madam Bond.

"Well, I will tell them a different story," replied her son, "for you have been a faithful and affectionate mother to your fatherless children, and they both call you blessed, to-day."

CHAPTER IX.

FOR months the blinds of Morning-Gleam Cottage were closed and its doors barred; silence, deeper than that called for by the voice of sickness, reigned through its halls and chambers. One of its inhabitants—she who had been its light and fairest ornament—lay sleeping beneath the pure marble erected to speak her praise by a weeping, bereaved church. Another, "cast down but not destroyed,"—he who had pointed many a bleeding heart to the great Healer—had been long months in foreign lands seeking health, a boon he never was to find until he reached the land where none shall say, "I am sick." The darling of the cottage was now the darling of a costly city mansion, far away from the little family-cemetery which overlooked Morning-Gleam. But the dear wanderer over the seas was not forgotten, nor yet forgotten was the green corner where slept the beloved. One little willow already dropped its lithe branches over the headstone.

The months and seasons have flown, and Maggie Bond is fourteen years old; tall, strong, and, although far from handsome, possessing that mingling of tenderness and resoluteness in manner which makes the plainest lovely. That fourteenth anniversary of her birth Maggie and her family spent in a dear, sad spot, at a solemn task. The heart which had beat in love so many years for the people of his choice lay still before them on the bier, brought hither to be laid in his long sleep beside the beloved. Mr. Bond had reached his home to die with his mother, his sister, and his child.

When the last touch of the spade had smoothed the mound, a brother, by whose side he had long labored in the ministry, said, "Thanks be unto God who hath given us the victory through our Lord Jesus Christ," and pronounced the last "Amen." Then the weeping crowd withdrew, and the family were alone. "Uncle Percy," one of Nature's noblemen, had, in regard to Maggie's feelings, caused to be brought hither another tender willow, that her own hand might set it above her father's new-made grave.

"Did your parents make this as a request of you, my child?" asked her grandmother.

"They did not," replied she; "but my father suggested it once in impressing a certain duty on my mind—that of loving, and remembering, and obeying Jesus *in all things.* I hope I may be able, as long as I live, to add a willow to these two every year; thus keeping *them* in mind, I shall not feel like an orphan, nor homeless either, for this spot seems now like my own dwelling-place. Do you see, my dear, kind uncle bade the undertaker save a place for me between them?" and she gave Mr. Percy a look of gratitude which more than repaid him for all the trouble he had ever had through her. Maggie then related the conversation of her father in the grove above them, and told of the pledge she had given him, that she would ever in all things follow Jesus closely, through evil as well as good report. She spoke of his decided views of God's ordinances, and said, while tears coursed down her cheeks, "My only regret now is that before his death I had not made an open profession of my faith. It would have been a joy to him, having confidence in my conversion, to know that I was not ashamed to confess the Saviour publicly."

"And why did you not do so, my love?" asked Mrs. Percy. "I do hope your tenderness for your uncle's prejudices or mine did not deter you from a known duty. Although your poor auntie is not a Christian herself, Maggie darling, she wants those who are blessed by being so to be consistent and faithful."

"It was just that very tenderness toward you all which hindered me from joining God's people when I found a hope in his mercy. I felt so utterly alone in my sentiments that I waited till my dear father should return to perform this duty. I carried an orphan's heart in my bosom even then, and had not the spirit for any controversy about it. I must in this matter follow my conscience, and *here* it will lead me among very lowly folks; but," said Maggie, sitting down upon the grass and laying her hand on the fresh earth, "I must say here, once for all, that my choice is to suffer affliction and reproach—any thing —with those of God's people whom I believe to be the nearest akin to him in spirit and doctrine. I must join this new Baptist church."

"So you may, my love," said Mr. Percy; "and I am pained to think you should have worried yourself with any fears of argument or opposition. You can't please everybody, do your best. If you try to please me, you would be confirmed by Dr. Winslow; and if to gratify your grandmother, you would unite with Mr. Spencer's church. The best way is to follow the New Testament *as you understand it;* you have more good sense now than half the grown women I know. I have not your father's spiritual religion, I well know, my love, but I have common humanity enough to keep me from tyrannizing over anybody's conscience. When we go back I'll call on the pastor of the little new church with you, my dear."

"Oh, Uncle Percy, you are so dear and kind—so like a real father," said the orphan. "I hope I may in some way repay you all for your love to me."

"You do repay us every day, my darling," replied her uncle; "but night is coming on, dear, and mother will take cold. Let us leave the dear grove and go down to good, faithful Mrs. Bell's. We can ride up in the morning before the cars go, for a last look. Mother Bell will water the willow till its roots strike."

"Oh," said Maggie, weeping, "how many there are here who would gladly do it! The memory of the just is blessed here."

During all this conversation poor Madam

Bond, seated on a garden chair which some mourner had placed in the little enclosure, listened silently, the tears coursing down her faded cheeks. She, unused to tears, was blessed that she could shed them now that the great sorrow of her life had fallen upon her. True, she had buried her husband, a good and noble man, yet she was then young, strong and self-reliant; but now, when gray hairs were upon her and her strength failing, the strong staff and the beautiful rod on which, notwithstanding her apparent coldness, her spirit had leaned with the strong, pure trust which only a mother can feel in a good and noble son, was broken. There is for every mortal a time to weep, and with her that time had come; else had that strong heart broken with the throes of pent-up agony. She scarcely realized the theme on which the younger mourners talked; showing how deep must have been the grief which destroyed her power of controversy and overcame her bigotry. Mr. Percy offered her his arm tenderly, and she descended the hill, followed by her daughter and poor Maggie, both of whom turned round again and again to catch one more glimpse of those dear graves.

"How desolate to be in this great, wide world without a father to watch over me," said poor Maggie, almost choked with grief.

"I know it is so, my love; but you have *us* left, and we will do more for you than it was in their power to do," said her aunt.

"Oh, no; you won't pray for me, you won't watch over me lest I wound Christ; you won't warn me against the temptations of an ungodly world!"

Mrs. Percy was silent a moment, and then she said, in a subdued tone, "Grandma will, my love."

"But in such a different way from that which *they* used to take; but I shall try to yield to her views as far as I can, for I promised my father in his last hour never to leave her, but to make her as happy as I possibly could. But really, dear auntie, I feel so truly orphaned to-day, that it seems as if a very little harshness would crush me."

"Darling," cried the noble woman, "your Uncle Percy has a perfect way of managing grandma! He will see that she is satisfied without suffering you to be even wounded—*crushed* you shall never be."

"My uncle is the most wonderful man I ever met," said Maggie. "Were it not for his extreme devotion to business and his love of pleasure, I should think he must be a Christian; but I know he is not."

"No, my dear child, neither of us has the hope you enjoy; and I can say, as you do, Maggie, that my chief pang, standing over those dear buried hearts, is that I have them no longer to pray for me. I used to feel such confidence that God heard them, and would, *for their sake,* save me in the hour of death But they will pray for us no more."

"Oh, auntie, did you never want to feel that you were one of the saved till the hour of death?" asked the little girl.

I want, at any rate, to *die* a Christian," said the lady. "That is, you know, the most important thing."

"No, no, I cannot feel it so," answered Maggie. "It seems to me the most important to have God honored and Christ glorified. In doing that we shall be blest with joy here and life beyond. I wish to remember what my dear, precious father said to me a few days before he went to heaven: 'My daughter, take care that you do not perform duty and seek after holiness with an eye single to your own happiness. Many young converts talk as if they had chosen Christ as their portion only as, were they less transitory, they would have chosen earthly pleasures. They read, pray, think, and labor, that a consciousness of having *done all* may bring a spirit of content and with it real pleasure. Here is danger of a self-righteous spirit gaining the ascendency, and we, instead of laboring for the coming of God's kingdom, toil only for the salvation of ourselves and those dear to us, which is but another form of selfishness.' I do want to serve God with grandmà, and you, and uncle, that HE may be glorified."

"What a dear, good child you are!" responded Mrs. Percy.

"No, I am not, auntie, and it makes me wretched when you and uncle say so; for, when my heart seems so unlike the heart of Jesus, I feel as if I were living a hypocrite's life before you. Please never tell me that again."

Mrs. Percy bent over Maggie and said, in a subdued tone, as if she half expected a rebuke, "How can it be that you are such a sinner? I cannot believe it, and I find myself, since your father's prayers for me have ceased, throwing myself on yours."

"On mine! Oh, auntie, you make me tremble. I who have so little faith—who cannot help myself—how shall I bear such a burden on my soul? Don't leave it there, but pray for yourself," said, the child.

"I do raise a sort of prayer, but I never

feel that I am heard," said the lady. "Oh, that dreadful night, when death was doing his work in the next chamber! I really felt his sting in my own soul, and I was in anguish because such a monster was in my dwelling, and he who would have shielded us by his prayers would pray for us no more. I tried to pray; but in a moment I thought of you and grew calm. I thought then 'of such is the kingdom of heaven,' and for her sake we shall be kept."

"Oh, my dear auntie," cried the child, "if I am to stand between you and the displeasure of God I shall be crushed. I hope, if reliance on a poor, weak child is to keep you from Christ, that very soon I may fill that little spot between those we love."

"Dry up your tears, my darling; see, uncle is looking at us, and he will blame me for allowing your thoughts to dwell on such sad themes. He greatly fears the trouble through which you have passed will dim your bright spirit, and you know we rely on you to make our home a cheerful one. Cheer up, dear, before we go in, for poor Auntie Bell seems heart-broken. She is now a widow and childless, so you must strive to comfort her. She loved your parents with a mother's love, and it will never be known on earth how much she sacrificed for them and for you, that your father might see this church stand where it does to-day. She is waiting us at the door."

"Dear, dear Auntie Bell!" cried Maggie, throwing her arms around her neck and bursting into tears. "Here is your poor orphan come to sleep once more in the little 'white room'—once more to say to you at bedtime,

'Now I lay me down to sleep.' "

No words were uttered now, all sitting in silence communing with their own hearts—some of them with heaven.

CHAPTER X.

IN the young city where Maggie's lot was cast, the Baptists had taken a good position. At the extreme end from Mr. Percy's residence was a strong church composed of people from abroad, many of whom had been pillars and ornaments to the temple from which they had come. This had recently sent off a "branch" to plant itself near them, hoping thus to gather in some of the plainer class who, in that aristocratic neighborhood, might be overlooked of others. To this chapel the child of many prayers found her way soon after her removal hither; and here she became deeply interested. Now it would have been far more in accordance with her uncle's views had she requested the horse to be harnessed, and the man kept from church to drive her down-town to the First Church; but he knew her spirit too well—he reverenced her principles too much to say so.

"Then am I to understand, Margaret," asked her grandmother one day, "that you are really going to forsake us all?"

"Nothing of the kind, dear grandmother," said the young girl.

"But you decide to join this feeble little Baptist church, don't you?"

"I do."

"You will find plenty of work there, let me warn you! In such struggling interests the labor falls on a few; the willing always being overburdened," replied the old lady.

"Oh, dear grandmother, I am so young and know so little and have nothing to give: nobody will think of looking to me as a burden-bearer."

"They are very good at planning," said madam. "Your uncle's porter is one of them—leads their choir, I believe. Of course he has told them that you are the daughter of a Baptist minister, and that, although you are poor, your uncle is not! They will save their own pockets by inveigling you into their church."

Maggie colored deeply, and laid down the knife and fork with which she had been eating her dessert. Mr. Percy saw the barbed arrow had pierced her sensitive heart, and in his own peculiar way strove to draw it out. He took his long, red purse from his pocket deliberately, and laid it down by his plate. He then commenced peeling an orange; but, looking up suddenly, asked Madam Bond:

"Who did you say was inveigling my little niece into mischief, mother?"

"I said these Baptists knew what they were doing when they made such efforts to inveigle her into their church," she repeated.

"Why, uncle dear," exclaimed Maggie, "not one effort has been made to induce me to go there. I almost felt wounded that no notice was taken of me for so long a time. I felt that a poor orphan in the weeds of woe ought to excite sympathy anywhere. I never spoke to the minister till the day you took me there."

"Mr. Percy took you there!" cried the old lady, bracing herself against the back of her chair. "What does she mean?"

"Oh, *we*—Maggie and I—called on this gentleman to have a little conversation with him; and we were so well pleased that we have about decided to become hearers of his. As to Maggie's poverty, it is pretty well balanced by my riches. So, if my porter told them I would give them something for her sake, I'll make him a true prophet. I hear their minister is not supported as he should be; so, next time you go to meeting there, give him that, my love, from your uncle," and he handed Maggie an eagle.

"*You* are not going to turn Baptist, are you, Mr. Percy?" asked Madam Bond.

"I think it more than probable; but I must turn *Christian* first or they will not have me. I never knew any of that denomination till I saw your son; but from my boy-

Morning Gleam.

PAGE 194.

hood up I have always wondered how those who professed to be governed by the New Testament could be any thing else. If I'm ever worthy to join any church, it will be a Baptist church. But aside from this, I do love to see people stand straight up for their own sentiments. If I were a Mormon, I'd own it, and not slip off into some more popular church. I honor everybody that is firm and consistent in his own faith."

"Ugh!" exclaimed grandma, "this people strain at a gnat and swallow a camel, do they not? You are so decided, Margaret, about being immersed because Jesus was—why don't you turn your back on all churches, because they do not worship in an upper-chamber, as he and his disciples did?"

"So I would, grandma, if he had *commanded us* to meet in an upper-chamber; but he has *not* done so," replied Maggie.

"Do you think God ever requires impossibilities of his creatures, my child?"

"No, ma'am, never."

"Well, then, suppose he had said, 'Believe and be baptized *in Jordan*:' what would you have done then?"

"I would have gone to Jordan," answered the young girl, artlessly.

"But that would be impossible," said Madam Bond.

"Not at all, grandma; people do go for mere pleasure; and I'm sure they could from a higher motive. But Jesus *has not* required this. He has removed every obstacle, and if we do not obey him, the blame must lie on ourselves."

"Well, my child, 'As the twig is bent the tree's inclined;' your parents certainly instructed and drilled you thoroughly in their peculiar views."

"Dear grandmother, they rarely ever alluded to this subject at home. It was *settled in their minds*. The first time I ever heard any talk about it was just before you came last to Morning-Gleam, and while you were there."

"Well, my love, I am not going to argue with you—old heads must bow before young ones in our day! You, ere you have reached your fifteenth year, have outstripped in research and in wisdom not only your poor superannuated grandmother, but also hosts of the wise and good of the present and of bygone ages! You know more than the ancients!"

Maggie could endure any thing but sarcasm; that was a spirit never breathed where she had lived, and armed with a strange sting it struck her to the very heart. With a quivering lip, expressive of deep pain rather than of anger, she left her dessert almost untouched, and, without leave, for she could not speak to ask it, fled to her own chamber. This had often proved a blessed sanctuary to her, for there she had met and communed with God and felt herself not fatherless.

A long conversation ensued at the table, in which Mr. Percy justified in unqualified terms the position in which Maggie stood. "Mother" he said, "it seems strange for me, who profess no real interest in these things, to contend with *you* for liberty of conscience! Could you respect Maggie as you now do were she, for the sake of pleasing us, to act a false part?"

"Respect her? I can respect any child who has modesty enough to yield her judgment to that of her superiors in age and wisdom. I can't endure the thought of her breaking the family-chain by going down to that little chapel! The Baptists are such bigots they think nobody right but themselves!"

"Do you think any church right but your own?" asked Mr. Percy.

"No, sir!" exclaimed Madam Bond, "I do not!"

"Then why should you require more of other sects? If they thought any other organization nearer to the truth than their own, they would no longer be Baptists. My tastes are not satisfied with their own rigid simplicity; but I do believe they are very near to the church which our great Leader founded, whose main pillars were fishermen of Galilee."

"You amaze me, Mr. Percy."

"I'm sorry, mother; but I really have a great reverence for any people who dare to stand up boldly for their own sentiments when all is against them. These Baptists, toward whom you have so much feeling, are the only denomination which never persecuted others for conscience sake."

"Well, there is no use in talking," exclaimed Madam Bond, weeping. "I see just how it is: you and Caroline think me superannuated and losing my mental powers, so you choose to accept the judgment of a child before mine! I suppose poor, dear Endicott held the same views, and expressed them before Margaret."

"Oh, dear mother," said Mrs. Percy, in a soothing tone, "that is a great mistake. You have not changed a whit, but are as vigorous to-day as when I was a girl at home. I'm quite sure your ideas of the Baptists have not undergone any change since then. I think you felt the same when Endicott joined them."

Still the old lady wept, and poor Mrs. Percy, desiring the happiness of all, scarcely knew what course to pursue. The sight of tears from her mother's eyes was new to her; this being only the second time in her whole life she had ever seen her weeping. She spoke soothingly to her, as Mr. Percy withdrew to the little library, from which opened Maggie's room, to read his paper. After some time Mrs. Percy entered that room by another door and found her niece also in tears.

"Oh, Maggie, dear, do not cry; it makes me so miserable!" And seating herself on the side of the bed where Maggie lay, she drew the curly head upon her bosom and pressed *almost* a mother's kiss on the red lips of the child. "Now, dear, listen to me, who love you. You know how very rigid poor grandmother is in her views, and how unhappy she is when she is thwarted in her plans. She loves you dearly: you and I are all she has to love; she has nothing left to look forward to as we have—nothing but the grave. Now, my love, suppose you magnanimously resolve to give up your will to hers as long as she lives; that will be but a little while."

"What *do* you mean, auntie dear?" asked Maggie, in surprise.

"Why, my love, that you join grandma's church, and go with her," said Mrs. Percy.

"But, auntie dear, they would not take me unless I deceived them. Besides, I was not sprinkled when I was a baby."

"The minister would do it now, my love."

"Never!" said Maggie. "It would be mocking God."

"Oh, no, my dear," exclaimed Mrs. Percy. "You know it could not *hurt* you to have a little water put on your face."

"But I should do it in the name of an

ordinance of God, which *it is not;* and thus should wrong my own conscience, deceive others, and insult God."

"Grandma will not live long, and after she is gone you can join where you please," said the lady.

"I am unworthy enough of a place among God's people now, and I'm sure I should be more so then," said Maggie.

"I know grandma better than you do, love, and I know that with all her goodness she never yields a point to any one. She considers herself next to your own mother. If you go without her consent, you will have great trials, and it breaks my heart to think of any coldness or unkindness between you."

"Auntie, 'He that loveth father or mother more than me is not worthy of me.' I have resolved to obey Christ in all things as far as I possibly can; and if that brings sorrow and unkindness with it, I must just receive that as a part of my discipline at his hand. If you or Uncle Percy or grandma say in so many words that *I shall not be baptized,* I shall wait, for I am under your control; but nothing short of this will keep me back."

"*I* should not dare to say so, love; and your uncle really thinks you ought to follow your own judgment in the matter: I am afraid to lay the whole responsibility on grandma, lest she readily take it up and forbid you. She is not afraid of such burdens."

"I hope you will *not* leave the decision with her, my dear aunt. I feel that it would almost be cruel toward me. I could bear open persecution or unkindness far better than these fetters of love, which draw me back from duty. Just before you came in, I was thinking of the martyrs who went to the stake for Jesus, and I despised myself when I saw how mere frowns and cool words alarmed me. Auntie, I don't believe one is a real disciple of Jesus unless he is willing to endure some trial for his sake; and this afternoon I feel that in his strength I could go to the flames to testify of his love and faithfulness."

"My dear child!" exclaimed Mrs. Percy, looking at Maggie in amazement, "oh, how I wish I had your religion!"

A rustling of paper was heard in the next room, and Mr. Percy stood in the door. "Do you wish for Maggie's faith, my wife?" he asked, looking sadly on her.

"Indeed I do."

"Then, I beseech you, do not tempt *her* to sin by urging her to stifle conscience to please any mortal. I tell you, Caroline, that the child's resolute determination to serve God as she believes he requires has had more effect on me than all the sermons, prayers, and forms I ever heard or saw in my life! I have seen the power of a living principle, and am led to desire the same to light and warm my own heart. I have tried to rely on splendid forms and ceremonies, tried to be a skeptic, and disbelieve all that is holy; but her example has saved me. I believe Heaven in mercy sent her here to rebuke our worldliness, and to lead us to God. I am the head of this family and the guardian of Maggie. I am, to all intents and purposes, her father, and it is my will that no one interfere with her in this matter. I will take the responsibility, and if mother speaks to you again about it, my dear, refer her to me."

"What will she say?" asked Mrs. Percy.

"She will probably say we are all bigots; but we will allow her what we ask for others—the rights of conscience. I sincerely hope, my dear, that you will not allow yourself to be led into wrong against Maggie for the sake of peace. Make no allusion whatever to this subject, and as it is so distasteful to grandma she will not expect to be consulted. I will take care of Maggie, and you may go to church with mother next Sabbath. When it is over, I, myself, will break it to her."

Poor Mrs. Percy was by nature a peacemaker, and had become pretty perfect through practice; always having had to stand between some other party and her mother. She was so desirous of making all things agreeable that she was in danger of suffering wrong to be done. She now said, "Mother remarked, after you left the table, that if our dear little girl still persisted in her course, it would be quite an alleviation if she would go down-town to the *First Church.* She would then have something like society."

"That is a very mean sort of pride," replied the gentleman, "and I hope Maggie will do no such thing! It would be getting up a carriage and riding to church for the sake of popularity, when she can do far more good at her own door. Suppose, Caroline, that she do so and that every Baptist in respectable circumstances do the same, how long will it take to build up a good strong church in this growing neighborhood?"

"Well, well, you are right, my dear, and I will leave all in your hands; but I confess I am almost afraid to face mother at tea, for she thinks I have come to plead with Maggie."

"Maggie, my dear, it is settled now," said her uncle; "if any one wants to talk of this matter send them to me. Since we have conversed so much about it, I spoke to a certain friend on the subject. He said he had never had a thought about it, but considered it settled by his church—the Episcopal; but that he should like to know your arguments for immersion. I promised to ask you for them."

"My arguments!" said Maggie, "I haven't one! I never thought of arguments. Jesus sets the example, and I mean to follow: he commands, and I obey. Were this a misty subject, I might have looked for arguments; but in the New Testament it is as plain as the noonday sun, that *believers,* and they alone, are to be *buried with Christ in Baptism.* I believe, dear uncle, with my poor little French friend Pierre, that 'if no man ever hear of sprinkle and go to Testament alone, then no man ever sprinkle—not big one, not baby.' I believe any one willing and anxious to find out the truth may do so, for the Bible is not a book for the learned more than for the ignorant. A wayfaring man, though a fool, need not err in this. Dear father once told me that he thought words often darkened counsel where God speaks as plainly as he does on this duty. Send your friend to the word and to the testimony: that is all the guide any of us have. I shall never repay your noble generosity, my dear uncle, in this sore trial. You were my terror when I came. I thought your pride would be wounded by my intended course—that you would look on it as a whim, and consider me obstinate not to yield to grandma's wishes. But God has been better than my fears, and it makes me feel so strong to have you for my champion that I almost fear I shall not realize enough my dependence on Him who has raised up such a dear, noble friend for the orphan of his servant."

"Now let us go down and take grandma out to walk in the garden," said Mrs. Percy to her niece. "Dear old lady, we will do all we can to make her happy while we have her with us. I hope we shall not kill her by carrying out our principles."

"There's spirit enough left in mother to keep her alive if we all should become Mohammedans. I wonder if she could have felt worse if Maggie had turned her back on her father's God and become a gay belle, trifling away her precious life!" said Mr. Percy.

Oh, what stone of stumbling causes more to fall than the bitter persecution of one Christian by another? And for a man of the world to stand and look on while one child of God has another in the dust with his heel on his neck, and perchance to step in between them to prevent the stronger from crushing the weaker—is it not almost enough to shake his faith in all we profess? Better be the oppressed than the oppressor.

CHAPTER XI.

THE glorious Sabbath morning dawned with a joy more than earthly upon our little Maggie. The holy, blessed women who, long ago, were "last at the cross, first at the sepulchre," brought spices, on a morn like this, as a sweet offering to anoint the body of their dead Redeemer: on *this* day, she of whom we write came, in the dew of her youth, and laid herself on the altar, a living sacrifice, holy and acceptable. With every facility for earthly pleasure she turned her face toward those joys which are forevermore at God's right hand. She took his vows upon her, and became his by outward profession. Then, as in almost every case, the terrible clouds of persecution which she had seen before her all vanished; no peal of thunder broke, no flash of lightning sped over her; the sun shone forth in new beauty, and she went on her way rejoicing.

Poor grandma, when she heard that Maggie had really gone forward and professed her faith, by what alone she called baptism, only said, "I expected it would come to this, and am very glad you did not tell me until it was over! She is a sweet child, and possesses real religious principle. She is very obstinate; but I don't know as she ought to be censured for that, as it is in every drop of the Hale blood! They are such rigid Baptists! My dear Endicott, too, had that trait among his many virtues—where ever he got it: I know it was not from my family, the Brewsters!" When Maggie bid her friends "good-night" that Sabbath evening, grandma put both arms around her and said, "My dear child, I hope God will keep you from ever dishonoring his cause, and that he will bless you abundantly, now and forever."

These words were a sort of peace-offering,

which atoned for all the coldness of the past —a benediction at the close of a life's service —a sweet incense never to cease rising while Maggie lived—a treasure to be hoarded up among her jewels; for these were the last words poor Madam Bond intelligibly uttered on earth! During that night a stroke of palsy almost deprived her of her reason; and although she lived a long year after, it was both to her and to her family like the first year of a baby's life. She had so much of mind left as to know her own family from strangers; and would suffer none but Mrs. Percy or Maggie to attend her. No matter what kind friend volunteered her services, or what skillful nurse was employed, she would reach out her arms toward them with such a touching moan as went to their very hearts. They never both left her at once; one rested while the other watched and ministered. Now came to their aid this strong, resolute, unbending purpose; the same spirit which made Maggie a Baptist sustained her and kept her at her post of duty. Now was seen the wisdom of Maggie's rigid training, and the real value of a constitution strengthened by morning air and exercise. Had dear Grandmother Bond been permitted to rise from that bed, we believe it would have been with a heart full of love to all—full of charity toward even the Baptists! This was not to be; and at the close of this suffering year, as the fruit was being gathered, and as the reapers were binding their sheaves, she, too, was taken as a sheaf of corn fully ripe to the garner above.

Scarcely had the grave closed over the aged Christian ere a letter came from Auntie Bell, saying that Nancy Darby was lying at the house of her nephew in her last sickness; and that her only earthly desire was to see the child of her love. The journey was a long one, and Mr. and Mrs. Percy feared that Maggie's desire for usefulness might induce her to assume labors there again before she had recovered from those of the past. After much discussion it was agreed that they all should take the journey and return together. Aside from fulfilling a duty toward a faithful friend and servant, the place where Nancy lived had a strong claim on Maggie Bond: it was her birthplace, and it contained the graves of those she loved.

Nancy's pathway to the tomb was lighted by the presence and kindness of her friends. Hers was an illness which left the mind active and vigorous, while rapidly taking down, pin after pin, the poor tabernacle of clay. Once she said, "Oh, sometimes when I fall asleep, I dream I'm safe over, and that I have met your father and mother, and my mother, and lots more of the glorified on the shining shore; but when I wake up and find that I'm still the same poor Nancy Darby, and haven't got my glorified body, my poor heart aches. I'm homesick!"

"Well, my dear, good Nancy," said Maggie, "let me tell you what sweet words I read the other day in a German book. 'Blessed are the homesick, for they shall reach home.'"

"La, dear child!" cried Nancy in her old tones, "that is a new 'blessed,' for sure. I was a-trying to take some of the old ones to myself when my nephew's wife read them to me, but I couldn't. I wasn't 'pure in heart,' I wasn't 'meek,' I wasn't 'poor in sperrit,' I wasn't 'a peace-maker,' I wasn't 'persecuted.' But you have found a new 'blessed,' that I, poor, sinful Nancy Darby, can lay hold on. 'Blessed are the homesick:' I'm one of them, I know; so I shall reach home. But the nearer I get to God, the farther I seem from him—I mean the nearer I get to heaven, the more plain I see my sins; for I see him in all his holiness, and can say with Job, 'I have heard of thee by the hearing of the ear; but now mine eye seeth thee: therefore I abhor myself and repent in dust and ashes.' None of you that bore such heaps with me knowed what sins was hid and stowed away in my heart. Oh, if poor Madam Bond was here to-day, I'd have confessions to make to her! She wasn't an angel mor'n I was; but that's nothing to do with *my* sins. If a sinner saved by grace *can* hate a fellow cretur', then there's been times that I hated that old lady! She was harsh to my folks, and she despised the Baptises; but it was my duty to bear and forbear, to return good for evil, love for hatred; 'stead o' that, I always paid her back in her own coin. Now, beside the sin against God, I'm afraid—between us—she and I led them two sweet peace-makers, your father and mother, a terrible life on't. I'd like to confess to madam, but it's too late; so when I get to heaven she'll be the first earthly one I'll give my hand to. We'll both be tamed then."

"Nancy, you're talking too much," said Maggie.

"Well, I don't feel it, my child. It almost seems as if I was going to get about again; I feel so sort of lifted-up!"

"Nancy, my good girl"—she still called *herself* a girl—"if you do recover, you may come and spend your days with us, and take care of Maggie, or let her take care of you, just as you may agree about that, between you. I will give you a nice little room all to yourself, and take care of you in your old age," said Mrs. Percy.

"I feel as if I could walk there," said Nancy, "but I shall never see old age, nor I don't want to, neither! All my folks is in heaven, and I'd rather go there than even to live and be with our child. I'm a furrener and a stranger here, and long to go home. Oh, when I look back on the beautiful easy life I have had here, I feel amazed that God hadn't left me to settle down with earth for my portion; but he hasn't, blessed be his name ?"

This was one of the many conversations which passed between the faithful Nancy and her friend. Thus a week was spent under the shadow of Morning-Gleam. It was called now 'the parsonage' only, for Mr. Bond's successor was a practical man in the widest sense of the word, enough so to satisfy even farmer Grub. He had cut down the trees in the fine grove, and the limbs which erst spread their shadow and their beauty over the landscape lay dissevered and in a thousand pieces in the huge new wood-house, seasoning for the fuel of many a coming winter. The *useless flower-garden* was laid down to grass, and the strawberry beds to carrots. Oh, how Maggie's heart ached when she stood at the gate and looked around! She could not go in, as invited to do by the pastor's worthy wife. She rejoiced to know they were good and kind to their flock; but as she gazed on their out-door arrangements and saw their boys, she remembered Nancy's comments on them: "They're Christians, and the church is getting blest through 'em; but they are not *our kind of folks.* I heard *him* say more about the pigs he's raising for next winter's pork than ever I heard Mr. Bond say about eatables in all my life! But I'll forgive him, for he set out a little willow in our cemetery when he heard the old lady was sick and Maggie couldn't come."

At the end of the week the little party left

for a trip to the mountains; thence they went to the glory of our country—Niagara—and home again; expecting to hear from Auntie Bell if Nancy recovered so far as to follow them. Maggie felt it would be a sweet privilege to smooth her way to the silent land; but it was never to be. Soon after their departure she ended her lowly life in a peaceful death, requesting, with her last breath, to be laid, as Mr. Percy said she might be, in his enclosure. "Dig my grave in the farthest corner," she said. "I'm not worthy to lie so near their blessed dust; but oh, it will be sweet to *awake in the morning* and find us all again together." And there she sleeps.

* * * * * *

Once more in their home, the thoughts of Mr. and Mrs. Percy turned to Maggie's interests, and various plans were proposed by which to carry on her education. It was their desire to make her a thoroughly accomplished woman, such as should adorn their home and satisfy their pride; for they felt now how much of their happiness depended on her life and her future tastes. As to the method to be pursued—whether away at school or with teachers at home—she was consulted; for her happiness lay very near their hearts.

"Now, my love," said her uncle, one day, "you are released from the sick-room and from all care. It is time you resume the studies you dropped at Morning-Gleam. Where will you do it, and what branches will you pursue?"

"Uncle," replied the young girl, "my dear father spared no pains in laying the foundation of a sound education. I knew well, when a little child, the hopes he cherished for me; and it was these which led him through what grandma called the 'toughening process' with me. He wished me to be a *working-woman,* either at home or abroad. This remark I well remember hearing him make: 'Look for *work,* not for *rest;* it is only the weary who can enjoy rest.' I feel your kindness, and could live very happily here all my days; but I know it would not meet my father's wishes. He said he hoped I might do much for Christ which his short life prevented him from doing. And I want you and dear auntie to feel, in all you do for me, that you will not, in all probability, be personally benefited by it—that, after all your pains and expense, I may be called to toil on a foreign shore."

"Oh, but, my love, there are plenty of *poor girls* who would be glad to go abroad under the sanction of some Society," said Mrs. Percy. "We can never let *you* go. Uncle will give money, and those who cannot do that may give their children."

"And those," said Maggie, smiling, "who, like me, have neither money nor children, must give *themselves*. God may never appoint me to such an honorable place; but I wish to speak very plainly about my future course before my uncle spends his money on my education. *If God calls I shall obey.* I do not wish to

——'be carried to the skies
On flowery beds of ease,
While others fought to win the prize,
And sailed through bloody seas.'"

Her friends looked at each other and then at Maggie. Hers was a spirit they could not fathom.

"My child," said Mr. Percy, "I have been trying to loosen myself from this earth that I might grow a better man; but I fear now that I have been leaning on your goodness to help me carry out my plans. Perhaps the Almighty means to strip me of every earthly dependence and leave me alone face to face with himself. How can I endure it?"

"It is thus we must all stand, dear uncle, and if we look at God through the face of Jesus, our brother, we have no cause for terror," said Maggie.

"My love, pursue the course of study which you yourself think wisest for your future hopes; I shall be satisfied," said the noble man.

Maggie Bond is toiling in the harvest-field even now, while yet a school-girl. Her first efforts are for the loved ones at home, and for the humble members of her uncle's dwelling. Both Mr. and Mrs. Percy attend the little new church with Maggie, and manifest great interest in its welfare. They also seem seeking the path that leads to "life;" and yet may be verified in their case the prophecy,

"A little child shall lead them."

Long ere this generation of reapers fall with the sickle in their hand upon the shores of India, we may hear of Margaret Bond among their number. Her strong arm may yet sustain the weary head, her fine spirit uphold the sinking heart of some sister who has given her life to the heathen.

The Christian who, dying young, leaves to the church a well-trained and truly devoted child, does more for Christ than he who leaves his thousands for the cause. One who, for the sake of principle, obeying her Saviour's command literally, could break through the cords of love and bigotry as did Maggie Bond, will not be very likely to quail before hardship at home, at sea, or on the dark shores of heathenism. God give to the church more such fathers and mothers as were hers; God grant unto many parents such children as she: then shall the day break which is foretold of the prophet, when the wilderness shall blossom as the rose, and when nothing shall hurt or destroy in all the holy mountain.

www.ingramcontent.com/pod-product-compliance
Lightning Source LLC
LaVergne TN
LVHW050526100826
845148LV00002B/458